CROCK·POT®

· THE ORIGINAL SLOW COOKER ·

5 Ingredients

pil

Publications International, Ltd.

Pictured on the front cover: Italian Pot Roast with Mushrooms *(page 88)*.

Pictured on the back cover *(left to right):* Barley with Currants and Pine Nuts *(page 176),* Pineapple and Pork Teriyaki *(page 78)* and Oatmeal with Maple-Glazed Apples and Cranberries *(page 16).*

ISBN: 978-1-68022-897-7

Library of Congress Control Number: 2015935363

Manufactured in China.

8 7 6 5 4 3 2 1

Publications International, Ltd.

TABLE OF CONTENTS

SLOW COOKING TIPS

Sizes of CROCK-POT®
Slow Cookers

Smaller **CROCK-POT®** slow cookers—such as 1- to 3½-quart models—are the perfect size for cooking for singles, a couple or empty nesters (and also for serving dips).

While medium-size **CROCK-POT®** slow cookers (those holding somewhere between 3 quarts and 5 quarts) will easily cook enough food at a time to feed a small family. They are also convenient for holiday side dishes or appetizers.

Large **CROCK-POT®** slow cookers are great for large family dinners, holiday entertaining and potluck suppers. A 6- to 7-quart model is ideal if you like to make meals in advance, or have dinner tonight and store leftovers for another day.

Types of CROCK-POT®
Slow Cookers

Current **CROCK-POT®** slow cookers come equipped with many different features and benefits, from auto cook programs to oven-safe stoneware to timed programming. Please visit **WWW.CROCK-POT.COM** to find the **CROCK-POT®** slow cooker that best suits your needs.

How you plan to use a **CROCK-POT®** slow cooker may affect the model you choose to purchase. For everyday cooking, choose a size large enough to serve your family. If you plan to use the **CROCK-POT®** slow cooker primarily for entertaining, choose one of the larger sizes. Basic **CROCK-POT®** slow cookers can hold as little as 16 ounces or as much as 7 quarts. The smallest sizes are great for keeping dips warm on a buffet, while the larger sizes can more readily fit large quantities of food and larger roasts.

Cooking, Stirring and Food Safety

CROCK-POT® slow cookers are safe to leave unattended. The outer heating base may get hot as it cooks, but it should not pose a fire hazard. The heating element in the heating base functions at a low wattage and is safe for your countertops.

Your **CROCK-POT®** slow cooker should be filled about one-half to three-fourths full for most recipes unless otherwise instructed. Lean meats such as chicken or pork tenderloin will cook faster than meats with more connective tissue and fat such as beef chuck or pork shoulder. Bone-in meats will take longer than boneless cuts. Typical **CROCK-POT®** slow cooker dishes take approximately 7 to 8 hours to reach the simmer point on LOW and about 3 to 4 hours on HIGH. Once the vegetables and meat start to simmer and braise, their flavors will fully blend and meat will become fall-off-the-bone tender.

According to the U.S. Department of Agriculture, all bacteria are killed at a temperature of 165°F. It's important to follow the recommended cooking times and not to open the lid often, especially early in the cooking process when heat is building up inside the unit. If you need to open the lid to check on your food or are adding additional ingredients, remember to allow additional cooking time if necessary to ensure food is cooked through and tender.

Large **CROCK-POT®** slow cookers, the 6- to 7-quart sizes, may benefit from a quick stir halfway through cook time to help distribute heat and promote even cooking. It's usually unnecessary to stir at all, as even ½ cup liquid will help to distribute heat and the stoneware is the perfect medium for holding food at an even temperature throughout the cooking process.

Oven-Safe Stoneware

All **CROCK-POT®** slow cooker removable stoneware inserts may (without their lids) be used safely in ovens at up to 400°F. In addition, all **CROCK-POT®** slow cookers are microwavable without their lids. If you own another slow cooker brand, please refer to your owner's manual for specific stoneware cooking medium tolerances.

Frozen Food

Frozen food can be successfully cooked in a **CROCK-POT®** slow cooker. However, it will require longer cooking time than the same recipe made with fresh food. It is almost always preferable to thaw frozen food prior to placing it in the **CROCK-POT®** slow cooker. Using an instant-read thermometer is recommended to ensure meat is fully cooked through.

Pasta and Rice

If you are converting a recipe for a **CROCK-POT®** slow cooker that calls for uncooked pasta, first cook the pasta on the stovetop just until slightly tender. Then add the pasta to the **CROCK-POT®** slow cooker. If you are converting a recipe for the **CROCK-POT®** slow

cooker that calls for cooked rice, stir in raw rice with the other recipe ingredients plus ¼ cup extra liquid per ¼ cup of raw rice.

Beans

Beans must be softened completely before combining with sugar and/or acidic foods in the **CROCK-POT®** slow cooker. Sugar and acid have a hardening effect on beans and will prevent softening. Fully cooked canned beans may be used as a substitute for dried beans.

Vegetables

Root vegetables often cook more slowly than meat. Cut vegetables accordingly to cook at the same rate as meat—large or small or lean versus marbled—and place near the sides or bottom of the stoneware to facilitate cooking.

Herbs

Fresh herbs add flavor and color when added at the end of the cooking cycle; if added at the beginning, many fresh herbs' flavor will dissipate over long cook times. Ground and/or dried herbs and spices work well in slow cooking and may be added at the beginning of cook time. For dishes with shorter cook times, hearty fresh herbs such as rosemary and thyme hold up well. The flavor power of all herbs and spices can vary greatly depending on their particular strength and shelf life. Use chili powders and garlic powder sparingly, as these can sometimes intensify over the long cook times. Always taste the finished dish and correct seasonings including salt and pepper.

page 102

Liquids

It's not necessary to use more than ½ to 1 cup liquid in most instances since juices in meats and vegetables are retained more in slow cooking than in conventional cooking. Excess liquid can be cooked down and concentrated after slow cooking on the stovetop or by removing meat and vegetables from stoneware, stirring in one of the following thickeners and setting the **CROCK-POT®** slow cooker to HIGH. Cover; cook on HIGH for approximately 15 minutes or until juices are thickened.

FLOUR: All-purpose flour is often used to thicken soups or stews. Stir cold water into the flour in a small bowl until smooth. With the **CROCK-POT®** slow cooker on HIGH, whisk the flour mixture into the liquid in the **CROCK-POT®** slow cooker. Cover; cook on HIGH 15 minutes or until the mixture is thickened.

page 178

CORNSTARCH: Cornstarch gives sauces a clear, shiny appearance; it's used most often for sweet dessert sauces and stir-fry sauces. Stir cold water into the cornstarch in a small bowl until the cornstarch dissolves. Quickly stir this mixture into the liquid in the **CROCK-POT®** slow cooker; the sauce will thicken as soon as the liquid simmers. Cornstarch breaks down with too much heat, so never add it at the beginning of the slow cooking process and turn off the heat as soon as the sauce thickens.

ARROWROOT: Arrowroot (or arrowroot flour) comes from the root of a tropical plant that is dried and ground to a powder; it produces a thick, clear sauce. Those who are allergic to wheat often use it in place of flour. Place arrowroot in a small bowl or cup and stir in cold water until the mixture is smooth. Quickly stir this mixture into the liquid in the **CROCK-POT®** slow cooker. Arrowroot thickens below the boiling point, so it even works well in a **CROCK-POT®** slow cooker on LOW. Too much stirring can break down an arrowroot mixture.

TAPIOCA: Tapioca is a starchy substance extracted from the root of the cassava plant. Its greatest advantage is that it withstands long cooking, making it an ideal choice for slow cooking. Add it at the beginning of cooking and you'll get a clear, thickened sauce in the finished dish. Dishes using tapioca as a thickener are best cooked on the LOW setting; tapioca may become stringy when boiled for a long time.

Milk

Milk, cream and sour cream break down during extended cooking. When possible, add them during the last 15 to 30 minutes of slow cooking, until just heated through. Condensed soups may be substituted for milk and may cook for extended times.

page 86

Fish

Fish is delicate and should be stirred into the **CROCK-POT®** slow cooker gently during the last 15 to 30 minutes of cooking time. Cover; cook just until cooked through and serve immediately.

page 20

Baked Goods

If you wish to prepare bread, cakes or pudding cakes in a **CROCK-POT®** slow cooker, you may want to purchase a covered, vented metal cake pan accessory for your **CROCK-POT®** slow cooker. You can also use any straight-sided soufflé dish or deep cake pan that will fit into the stoneware of your unit. Baked goods can be prepared directly in the stoneware; however, they can be a little difficult to remove from the insert, so follow the recipe directions carefully.

CROCK-POT® Slow Cooker Recipes with 5 Ingredients or Less

A well-stocked pantry is a shortcut to preparing dishes and entire meals efficiently. The five chapters in this cookbook take full advantage of the kinds of everyday ingredients most cooks commonly have on hand. They feature recipes that can be created with 5 ingredients and/or the addition of these common pantry items:

- Water

- Milk

- Butter

- Vegetable oil

- Olive oil

- Salt and black pepper

- Other common spices
(such as ground cinnamon, ground nutmeg, ground red pepper, red pepper flakes, garlic powder, ground cumin, ground oregano, dried thyme, chili powder, paprika, etc.)

- All-purpose flour

- Cornstarch

- Arrowroot

- Tapioca

- Granulated sugar

These slow-cooked recipes are perfect for busy days when you don't have time to make another stop at the grocery store.

MORNING TREATS

Maple, Bacon and Raspberry Pancake

5 slices bacon

2 cups pancake mix

1 cup water

½ cup maple syrup, plus additional for serving

1 cup fresh raspberries

3 tablespoons chopped pecans, toasted*

*To toast pecans, spread in a single layer in heavy skillet. Cook over medium heat 1 to 2 minutes or until nuts are lightly browned, stirring frequently.

1. Heat large skillet over medium heat. Add bacon; cook 7 to 8 minutes or until crisp. Remove to paper-towel lined plate; crumble.

2. Brush inside of 4- to 5-quart oval **CROCK-POT**® slow cooker with 1 to 2 tablespoons bacon fat from skillet. Combine pancake mix, water and ½ cup syrup in large bowl; stir to blend. Pour half of batter into **CROCK-POT**® slow cooker; top with half of raspberries, half of bacon and half of pecans. Pour remaining half of batter over top; sprinkle with remaining raspberries, bacon and pecans.

3. Cover; cook on HIGH 1½ to 2 hours or until pancake has risen and is cooked through. Turn off heat. Let stand, uncovered, 10 to 15 minutes. Remove pancake from **CROCK-POT**® slow cooker; cut into eight pieces. Serve with additional syrup.

Makes 8 servings

Ginger Pear Cider

8 cups pear juice or cider

¾ cup lemon juice

¼ to ½ cup honey

10 whole cloves

2 whole cinnamon sticks, plus additional for garnish

8 slices fresh ginger

1. Combine pear juice, lemon juice, honey, cloves, 2 cinnamon sticks and ginger in 5-quart **CROCK-POT®** slow cooker.

2. Cover; cook on LOW 5 to 6 hours or on HIGH 2½ to 3 hours. Remove and discard cloves, cinnamon sticks and ginger before serving. Garnish with additional cinnamon sticks.

Makes 8 to 10 servings

Whoa Breakfast

3 cups water

2 cups chopped peeled apples

1½ cups steel-cut or old-fashioned oats

¼ cup sliced almonds

½ teaspoon ground cinnamon

Combine water, apples, oats, almonds and cinnamon in **CROCK-POT®** slow cooker. Cover; cook on LOW 8 hours.

Makes 6 servings

Ginger Pear Cider

Banana Nut Bread

⅓ cup butter

3 mashed bananas

⅔ cup sugar

2 eggs, beaten

2 tablespoons dark corn syrup

1¾ cups all-purpose flour

2 teaspoons baking powder

½ teaspoon salt

¼ teaspoon baking soda

½ cup chopped walnuts

1. Grease and flour inside of **CROCK-POT**® slow cooker. Beat butter in large bowl with electric mixer at medium speed until fluffy. Gradually beat in bananas, sugar, eggs and corn syrup until smooth.

2. Combine flour, baking powder, salt and baking soda in small bowl; stir to blend. Beat flour mixture into banana mixture. Add walnuts; mix thoroughly. Pour batter into **CROCK-POT**® slow cooker.

3. Cover; cook on HIGH 2 to 3 hours. Cool completely; turn bread out onto large serving platter.

Makes 1 loaf

Tip: Banana Nut Bread has always been a favorite way to use up those overripe bananas. Not only is it delicious, but it also freezes well for future use.

Banana Nut Bread

Oatmeal with Maple-Glazed Apples and Cranberries

3 cups water

2 cups quick-cooking or old-fashioned oats

¼ teaspoon salt

1 teaspoon unsalted butter

2 medium red or Golden Delicious apples, unpeeled and cut into ½-inch pieces

¼ teaspoon ground cinnamon

2 tablespoons maple syrup

4 tablespoons dried cranberries

1. Combine water, oats and salt in **CROCK-POT**® slow cooker. Cover; cook on LOW 8 hours.

2. Melt butter in large nonstick skillet over medium heat. Add apples and cinnamon; cook and stir 4 to 5 minutes or until tender. Stir in syrup; heat through.

3. Serve oatmeal with apple mixture and dried cranberries.

Makes 4 servings

Tip: For a quick, make-ahead breakfast, freeze this oatmeal in individual portions. It can be reheated quickly in the microwave, saving the fuss of measuring, cooking and cleaning up.

Oatmeal with Maple-Glazed
Apples and Cranberries

Cinnamon-Ginger Poached Pears

3 cups water

1 cup sugar

10 slices fresh ginger

2 whole cinnamon sticks

1 tablespoon chopped
candied ginger (optional)

6 Bosc or Anjou pears, peeled
and cored

1. Combine water, sugar, ginger, cinnamon and candied ginger, if desired, in **CROCK-POT**® slow cooker. Add pears. Cover; cook on LOW 4 to 6 hours or on HIGH 1½ to 2 hours.

2. Remove pears with slotted spoon. Cook syrup, uncovered, on HIGH 30 minutes or until thickened. Remove and discard cinnamon sticks.

Makes 6 servings

Mucho Mocha Cocoa

4 cups whole milk

4 cups half-and-half

1 cup chocolate syrup

⅓ cup instant coffee granules

2 tablespoons sugar

2 whole cinnamon sticks

1. Combine milk, half-and-half, chocolate syrup, coffee granules, sugar and cinnamon sticks in **CROCK-POT**® slow cooker; stir to blend. Cover; cook on LOW 3 hours.

2. Remove and discard cinnamon sticks. Serve warm in mugs.

Makes 9 servings

Cinnamon-Ginger
Poached Pears

Orange Date Nut Bread

2 cups all-purpose flour, plus additional for dusting

½ cup chopped pecans

1 teaspoon baking powder

½ teaspoon baking soda

¼ teaspoon salt

1 cup chopped dates

2 teaspoons orange peel

⅔ cup boiling water

¾ cup sugar

2 tablespoons shortening

1 egg, lightly beaten

1 teaspoon vanilla

1. Spray 1-quart soufflé dish, casserole or other high-sided baking dish with nonstick cooking spray; dust with flour.

2. Combine 2 cups flour, pecans, baking powder, baking soda and salt in medium bowl.

3. Combine dates and orange peel in separate medium bowl; pour boiling water over date mixture. Add sugar, shortening, egg and vanilla; stir just until blended.

4. Add flour mixture to date mixture; stir just until blended. Pour batter into prepared dish; place in 4½-quart **CROCK-POT**® slow cooker. Cover; cook on HIGH 2½ hours or until edge begins to brown.

5. Remove dish from **CROCK-POT**® slow cooker. Cool on wire rack 10 minutes. Remove bread from dish; cool completely on wire rack.

Makes 10 servings

Variation: Substitute 1 cup dried cranberries for dates.

Orange Date Nut Bread

Apple and Granola Breakfast Cobbler

4 Granny Smith apples, peeled, cored and sliced

½ cup packed light brown sugar

1 tablespoon lemon juice

1 teaspoon ground cinnamon

2 cups granola cereal, plus additional for garnish

2 tablespoons butter, cut into small pieces

Whipping cream, half-and-half or vanilla yogurt (optional)

1. Place apples in **CROCK-POT**® slow cooker. Sprinkle brown sugar, lemon juice and cinnamon over apples. Stir in 2 cups granola and butter.

2. Cover; cook on LOW 6 hours or on HIGH 2 to 3 hours. Serve warm with additional granola sprinkled on top. Serve with cream, if desired.

Makes 4 servings

Spiced Citrus Tea

4 tea bags

Peel of 1 orange

4 cups boiling water

2 cans (6 ounces *each*) orange-pineapple juice

3 tablespoons honey

3 whole cinnamon sticks

3 star anise

1. Place tea bags, orange peel and boiling water in **CROCK-POT**® slow cooker; cover and let steep 10 minutes. Remove and discard tea bags and orange peel. Add juice, honey, cinnamon sticks and star anise.

2. Cover; cook on LOW 3 hours. Remove and discard cinnamon sticks and star anise.

Makes 6 servings

Apple and Granola
Breakfast Cobbler

Breakfast Quinoa

1½ cups uncooked quinoa

3 cups water

3 tablespoons packed brown sugar

2 tablespoons maple syrup

1½ teaspoons ground cinnamon

¾ cup golden raisins

Fresh raspberries and banana slices

1. Place quinoa in fine-mesh strainer; rinse well under cold running water. Remove to **CROCK-POT**® slow cooker.

2. Stir water, brown sugar, syrup and cinnamon into **CROCK-POT**® slow cooker. Cover; cook on LOW 5 hours or on HIGH 2½ hours or until quinoa is tender and water is absorbed.

3. Add raisins during last 10 to 15 minutes of cooking time. Top quinoa with raspberries and bananas.

Makes 6 servings

Apple Butter

3 pounds cooking apples, peeled and evenly sliced

2 cups sugar

1 tablespoon ground cinnamon

1 teaspoon ground ginger

1 teaspoon ground nutmeg

Combine apples, sugar, cinnamon, ginger and nutmeg in **CROCK-POT**® slow cooker. Cover; cook on LOW 8 hours or until thickened, stirring occasionally to break up any apple pieces.

Makes 5 cups

Breakfast Quinoa

Zucchini Bread

1⅔ cups all-purpose flour, plus
    additional for dusting

1¼ teaspoons ground cinnamon

1 teaspoon baking powder

½ teaspoon salt

½ teaspoon ground allspice

¼ teaspoon baking soda

1 cup sugar

2 eggs, lightly beaten

½ cup canola oil

1 tablespoon vanilla

1 large zucchini, trimmed
    and shredded

½ cup chopped walnuts

1. Spray inside of 8½×4½×2¾-inch ovenproof glass or ceramic loaf pan* that fits inside of **CROCK-POT**® slow cooker with nonstick cooking spray; dust with flour.

2. Combine 1⅔ cups flour, cinnamon, baking powder, salt, allspice and baking soda in medium bowl; stir to blend. Whisk sugar, eggs, oil and vanilla in another medium bowl. Pour sugar mixture into flour mixture; stir until just moistened. Gently fold in zucchini and walnuts. Pour into prepared loaf pan. Place in **CROCK-POT**® slow cooker. Cover; cook on HIGH 3½ to 3¾ hours or until toothpick inserted into center comes out clean.

3. Remove bread from **CROCK-POT**® slow cooker; let cool in pan 10 minutes. Remove bread from pan; let cool on wire rack 30 minutes before slicing.

Makes 1 loaf

*You may also use a glass bowl that fits inside of the **CROCK-POT**® slow cooker.*

Zucchini Bread

Viennese Coffee

3 cups strong freshly brewed
   hot coffee

3 tablespoons chocolate syrup

1 teaspoon sugar

⅓ cup whipping cream, plus
   additional for topping

¼ cup crème de cacao or Irish
   cream

Chocolate shavings
   (optional)

1. Combine coffee, chocolate syrup and sugar in **CROCK-POT®** slow cooker. Cover; cook on LOW 2 to 2½ hours.

2. Stir ⅓ cup whipping cream and crème de cacao into **CROCK-POT®** slow cooker. Cover; cook on LOW 30 minutes or until heated through. Ladle coffee into coffee cups. Top with additional whipped cream and chocolate shavings, if desired.

Makes 4 servings

Bacon and Cheese Brunch Potatoes

3 medium russet potatoes
   (about 2 pounds), peeled
   and cut into 1-inch cubes

1 cup chopped onion

½ teaspoon seasoned salt

4 slices bacon, crisp-cooked
   and crumbled

1 cup (4 ounces) shredded
   sharp Cheddar cheese

1 tablespoon water

1. Coat inside of **CROCK-POT®** slow cooker with nonstick cooking spray. Place half of potatoes in **CROCK-POT®** slow cooker. Sprinkle half of onion and seasoned salt over potatoes; top with half of bacon and cheese. Repeat layers. Sprinkle water over top.

2. Cover; cook on LOW 6 hours or on HIGH 3½ hours or until potatoes and onion are tender. Stir gently to mix; serve warm.

Makes 6 servings

Viennese Coffee

Blueberry-Banana Pancakes

2 cups all-purpose flour

⅓ cup sugar

1 tablespoon baking powder

½ teaspoon baking soda

½ teaspoon salt

½ teaspoon ground cinnamon

1¾ cups milk

2 eggs, lightly beaten

¼ cup (½ stick) unsalted butter, melted

1 teaspoon vanilla

1 cup fresh blueberries

2 small bananas, sliced (optional)

Maple syrup (optional)

1. Combine flour, sugar, baking powder, baking soda, salt and cinnamon in medium bowl; stir to blend. Combine milk, eggs, butter and vanilla in separate medium bowl; stir to blend. Pour milk mixture into flour mixture; stir until moistened. Gently fold in blueberries until combined.

2. Coat inside of **CROCK-POT**® slow cooker with nonstick cooking spray. Remove batter to **CROCK-POT**® slow cooker. Cover; cook on HIGH 2 hours or until puffed and toothpick inserted into center comes out clean. Cut into wedges; top with bananas and syrup, if desired.

Makes 8 servings

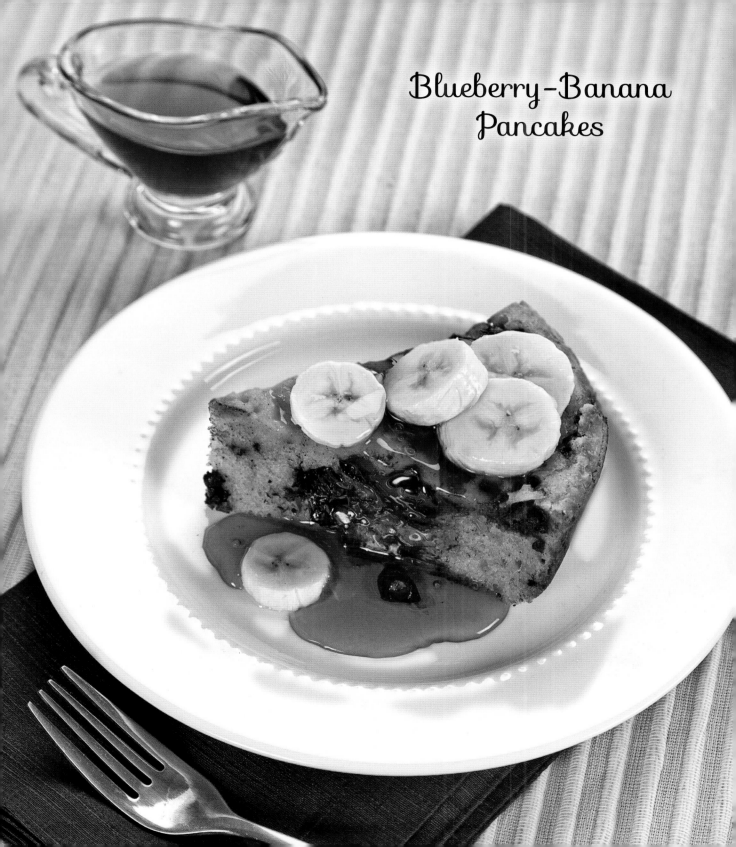

Blueberry-Banana
Pancakes

Chai Tea

2 quarts (8 cups) water

8 black tea bags

¾ cup sugar*

8 slices fresh ginger

5 whole cinnamon sticks, plus
additional for garnish

16 whole cloves

16 whole cardamom seeds,
pods removed (optional)

1 cup milk

*Chai tea is typically sweet. For less-sweet
tea, reduce sugar to ½ cup.*

1. Combine water, tea bags, sugar, ginger, 5 cinnamon sticks, cloves
and cardamom, if desired, in **CROCK-POT**® slow cooker; stir to blend.
Cover; cook on HIGH 2 to 2½ hours.

2. Strain mixture; discard solids. (At this point, tea may be covered
and refrigerated up to 3 days.)

3. Stir in milk just before serving. Garnish with additional cinnamon
sticks.

Makes 8 to 10 servings

MORNING TREATS

Chai Tea

Spiced Vanilla Applesauce

5 pounds (about 10 medium) sweet apples (such as Fuji or Gala), peeled and cut into 1-inch pieces

½ cup water

2 teaspoons vanilla

1 teaspoon ground cinnamon

¼ teaspoon ground nutmeg

¼ teaspoon ground cloves

1. Combine apples, water, vanilla, cinnamon, nutmeg and cloves in **CROCK-POT** slow cooker; stir to blend. Cover; cook on HIGH 3 to 4 hours or until apples are very tender.

2. Turn off heat. Mash mixture with potato masher to smooth out any large lumps. Let cool completely before serving.

Makes 6 cups

Cinnamon Roll-Topped Mixed Berry Cobbler

2 bags (12 ounces *each*) frozen mixed berries, thawed

1 cup sugar

¼ cup quick-cooking tapioca

¼ cup water

2 teaspoons vanilla

1 package (about 12 ounces) refrigerated cinnamon rolls with icing

Combine berries, sugar, tapioca, water and vanilla in **CROCK-POT** slow cooker; top with cinnamon rolls. Cover; cook on LOW 4 to 5 hours. Serve warm, drizzled with icing.

Makes 8 servings

Note: This recipe was designed to work best in a 4-quart **CROCK-POT** slow cooker. Double the ingredients for larger **CROCK-POT** slow cookers, but always place cinnamon rolls in a single layer.

Spiced Vanilla
Applesauce

Fresh Berry Compote

2 cups fresh blueberries

4 cups fresh sliced
   strawberries

2 tablespoons orange juice

½ to ¾ cup sugar

4 slices (½×1½ inches) lemon
   peel with no white pith

1 whole cinnamon stick
   or ½ teaspoon ground
   cinnamon

1. Place blueberries in **CROCK-POT**® slow cooker. Cover; cook on HIGH 45 minutes or until blueberries begin to soften.

2. Add strawberries, orange juice, ½ cup sugar, lemon peel and cinnamon stick; stir to blend. Cover; cook on HIGH 1 to 1½ hours or until strawberries are softened and sugar is dissolved. Check for sweetness and add more sugar, if necessary, cooking until added sugar is dissolved.

3. Remove insert from **CROCK-POT**® slow cooker to heatproof surface and let cool. Serve warm or chilled.

Makes 4 servings

Tip: To turn this compote into a fresh fruit topping for cake, ice cream, waffles or pancakes, carefully spoon out fruit, leaving cooking liquid in **CROCK-POT**® slow cooker. Stir ¼ cup cold water into 1 to 2 tablespoons cornstarch in small bowl until smooth; whisk into cooking liquid. Cover; cook on HIGH 10 to 15 minutes or until thickened. Return fruit to sauce; stir to blend.

Fresh Berry Compote

Wheat and Walnut Loaf

2 cups warm water (100° to 110°F), divided

¼ cup sugar

2 tablespoons vegetable oil

1 packet (¼ ounce) active dry yeast

2 cups all-purpose flour

1 cup whole wheat flour

⅔ cup walnut halves and pieces

1½ teaspoons salt

1. Combine 1 cup water, sugar, oil and yeast in small bowl; mix well. Let stand 5 minutes.

2. Combine flours, walnuts and salt in large bowl; stir to blend. Pour yeast mixture over flour mixture; stir until rough dough forms. Turn dough out onto floured surface; knead 6 to 7 minutes or until smooth and elastic. Place in 2½-quart ceramic baking dish. Cover with plastic wrap; let stand in warm place 30 minutes.

3. Place crumpled foil in bottom of 6-quart oval **CROCK-POT**® slow cooker. Pour in remaining 1 cup water. Remove plastic wrap from baking dish. Carefully place baking dish in **CROCK-POT**® slow cooker.

4. Cover; cook on HIGH 2¾ to 3 hours or until bread is cooked through and pulls away from sides. Remove bread from baking dish; let cool on wire rack 30 minutes.

Makes 1 loaf

Wheat and Walnut Loaf

Mocha Supreme

2 quarts strong brewed coffee

½ cup instant hot chocolate beverage mix

1 whole cinnamon stick, broken in half

1 cup whipping cream

1 tablespoon powdered sugar

1. Combine coffee, hot chocolate mix and cinnamon stick halves in **CROCK-POT**® slow cooker; stir to blend. Cover; cook on HIGH 2 to 2½ hours or until heated through. Remove and discard cinnamon stick halves.

2. Beat cream in medium bowl with electric mixer on high speed until soft peaks form. Add powdered sugar; beat until stiff peaks form. Ladle mocha mixture into mugs; top with whipped cream.

Makes 8 servings

Tip: To whip cream more quickly, chill the beaters and bowl in the freezer for 15 minutes.

Mocha Supreme

Ham and Potato Hash

1½ pounds red potatoes, sliced

8 ounces thinly sliced ham

2 poblano peppers, cut into thin strips

2 tablespoons olive oil

1 tablespoon dried oregano

¼ teaspoon salt

1 cup (4 ounces) shredded Monterey Jack or pepper jack cheese

2 tablespoons finely chopped fresh cilantro

1. Combine potatoes, ham, poblano peppers, oil, oregano and salt in **CROCK-POT®** slow cooker; stir to blend. Cover; cook on LOW 7 hours or on HIGH 4 hours.

2. Remove mixture to large serving platter; sprinkle with cheese and cilantro. Let stand 3 minutes or until cheese is melted.

Makes 6 to 7 servings

Ham and Potato Hash

Raisin-Oat Quick Bread

1½ cups all-purpose flour, plus additional for dusting

⅔ cup old-fashioned oats

⅓ cup milk

4 teaspoons baking powder

1 teaspoon ground cinnamon

½ teaspoon salt

½ cup packed raisins

1 cup sugar

2 eggs, slightly beaten

½ cup (1 stick) unsalted butter, melted, plus additional for serving

1 teaspoon vanilla

1. Spray inside of ovenproof glass or ceramic loaf pan that fits inside of **CROCK-POT®** slow cooker with nonstick cooking spray; dust with flour.

2. Combine oats and milk in small bowl; let stand 10 minutes.

3. Meanwhile, combine 1½ cups flour, baking powder, cinnamon and salt in large bowl; stir in raisins. Whisk sugar, eggs, ½ cup butter and vanilla in separate medium bowl; stir in oat mixture. Pour sugar mixture into flour mixture; stir just until moistened. Pour into prepared pan. Place in **CROCK-POT®** slow cooker. Cover; cook on HIGH 2½ to 3 hours or until toothpick inserted into center comes out clean.

4. Remove bread from **CROCK-POT®** slow cooker; let cool in pan 10 minutes. Remove bread from pan; let cool on wire rack 5 minutes before slicing. Serve with additional butter, if desired.

Makes 1 loaf

Raisin-Oat Quick Bread

ASIAN FLAVORS

Hoisin Sriracha Chicken Wings

3 pounds chicken wings, tips removed and split at joints

½ cup hoisin sauce, divided

¼ cup plus 1 tablespoon sriracha sauce, divided

2 tablespoons packed brown sugar

Sliced green onions (optional)

1. Coat inside of **CROCK-POT**® slow cooker with nonstick cooking spray. Preheat broiler. Spray large baking sheet with nonstick cooking spray. Arrange wings on prepared baking sheet. Broil 6 to 8 minutes or until browned, turning once. Remove wings to **CROCK-POT**® slow cooker.

2. Combine hoisin sauce, ¼ cup sriracha sauce and brown sugar in medium bowl; stir to blend. Pour sauce mixture over wings in **CROCK-POT**® slow cooker; stir to coat. Cover; cook on LOW 3½ to 4 hours. Remove wings to large serving platter; cover with foil to keep warm.

3. Turn **CROCK-POT**® slow cooker to HIGH. Cook, uncovered, on HIGH 10 to 15 minutes or until sauce is thickened. Stir in remaining 1 tablespoon sriracha sauce. Spoon sauce over wings to serve. Garnish with green onions.

Makes 5 to 6 servings

Steamed Pork Buns

½ (18-ounce) container refrigerated cooked shredded pork in barbecue sauce*

1 tablespoon Asian garlic chili sauce

1 package (about 16 ounces) refrigerated big biscuit dough (8 biscuits)

Dipping Sauce (recipe follows)

Sliced green onions (optional)

*Look for pork in plain, not smoky, barbecue sauce. Substitute chicken in barbecue sauce, if desired.

1. Combine pork and chili sauce in medium bowl; stir to blend. Split biscuits in half. Roll or stretch each biscuit into 4-inch circle. Spoon 1 tablespoon pork onto center of each biscuit. Gather edges around filling and press to seal.

2. Generously butter 2-quart baking dish that fits inside of 5- to 6-quart **CROCK-POT**® slow cooker. Arrange filled biscuits in single layer, overlapping slightly if necessary. Cover dish with buttered foil, butter side down.

3. Place small rack in **CROCK-POT**® slow cooker. Add 1 inch of hot water (water should not touch top of rack). Place baking dish on rack. Cover; cook on HIGH 2 hours.

4. Meanwhile, prepare Dipping Sauce. Garnish pork buns with green onions and serve with Dipping Sauce.

Makes 16 servings

Dipping Sauce: Stir together 2 tablespoons rice vinegar, 2 tablespoons soy sauce, 4 teaspoons sugar and 1 teaspoon toasted sesame oil in a small bowl until sugar dissolves. Sprinkle with 1 tablespoon minced green onion just before serving.

Tip: Straight-sided round casserole or soufflé dishes that fit inside the **CROCK-POT**® stoneware make excellent baking dishes.

Steamed Pork Buns

Vietnamese Chicken Pho

8 cups chicken broth

2 to 3 cups shredded cooked chicken

8 ounces bean sprouts

Rice stick noodles

1 bunch Thai basil, chopped

Hoisin sauce (optional)

Lime wedges (optional)

1. Combine broth and chicken in **CROCK-POT**® slow cooker. Cover; cook on LOW 6 to 7 hours or on HIGH 3 hours.

2. Add bean sprouts, noodles and Thai basil. Cover; cook on HIGH 20 minutes or until noodles are softened.

3. Spoon soup into individual serving bowls. Serve with hoisin sauce and lime wedges, if desired.

Makes 4 to 6 servings

Note: A simple soup to prepare with leftover shredded chicken, this classic Asian chicken noodle soup packs tons of flavor.

Vietnamese Chicken Pho

Asian Beef with Broccoli

1½ pounds boneless beef chuck roast (about 1½ inches thick), sliced into thin strips*

1 can (10½ ounces) condensed beef broth, undiluted

½ cup oyster sauce

2 tablespoons cornstarch

1 bag (16 ounces) fresh broccoli florets

Hot cooked rice

Sesame seeds (optional)

*Freeze steak 30 minutes to make slicing easier.

1. Place beef in **CROCK-POT**® slow cooker. Pour broth and oyster sauce over beef. Cover; cook on HIGH 3 hours.

2. Stir 2 tablespoons cooking liquid into cornstarch in small bowl until smooth; whisk into cooking liquid. Cover; cook on HIGH 15 minutes or until thickened.

3. Cook broccoli according to package directions. Add to **CROCK-POT**® slow cooker; toss gently. Serve with rice; garnish with sesame seeds.

Makes 4 to 6 servings

Asian Beef with Broccoli

Thai Chicken Wings

1 tablespoon peanut oil

5 pounds chicken wings, tips removed and split at joints

½ cup unsweetened canned coconut milk

1 tablespoon sugar

1 tablespoon Thai green curry paste

1 tablespoon fish sauce

¾ cup prepared spicy peanut sauce

Sliced green onions (optional)

1. Heat oil in large skillet over medium-high heat. Add wings in batches; cook 3 to 5 minutes or until browned on all sides. Remove to **CROCK-POT®** slow cooker using slotted spoon.

2. Stir coconut milk, sugar, curry paste and fish sauce into **CROCK-POT®** slow cooker. Cover; cook on LOW 6 to 7 hours or on HIGH 3 to 3½ hours. Remove wings with slotted spoon to large bowl; toss with peanut sauce before serving. Garnish with green onions.

Makes 8 to 10 servings

Thai Chicken Wings

Best Asian-Style Ribs

2 full racks pork baby back
 ribs, split into 3 sections
 each

6 ounces hoisin sauce

½ cup maraschino cherries,
 drained

½ cup rice wine vinegar

2 tablespoons minced fresh
 ginger

Combine ribs, hoisin sauce, cherries, vinegar and ginger in
CROCK-POT® slow cooker. Cover; cook on LOW 6 to 7 hours or
on HIGH 3 to 3½ hours.

Makes 6 to 8 servings

Tip: Baby back pork ribs are called "baby" because they are smaller than
spareribs. They're cut from the loin of the pig, cook in less time and are
more tender than spareribs.

Best Asian-Style Ribs

Curried Lentils with Fruit

5 cups water

1½ cups dried brown lentils,
    rinsed and sorted

1 Granny Smith apple,
    chopped, plus additional
    for garnish

¼ cup golden raisins

¼ cup lemon yogurt

1 teaspoon salt

1 teaspoon curry powder

1. Combine water, lentils, 1 chopped apple and raisins in **CROCK-POT**® slow cooker; stir to blend. Cover; cook on LOW 8 to 9 hours or until most liquid is absorbed.

2. Remove lentil mixture to large bowl; stir in yogurt, salt and curry powder until blended. Garnish with additional apple.

Makes 6 servings

Curried Lentils with Fruit

Spicy Orange Chicken Nuggets

1 bag (28 ounces) frozen popcorn chicken bites

1½ cups prepared honey teriyaki marinade

¾ cup orange juice concentrate

⅔ cup water

1 tablespoon orange marmalade

½ teaspoon hot chile sauce or sriracha*

Hot cooked rice with peas and corn

Sriracha is a Thai hot sauce and is available in Asian specialty markets and large supermarkets.

1. Preheat oven to 450°F. Spread chicken evenly on baking sheet. Bake 12 to 14 minutes or until crisp. (Do not brown.) Remove to **CROCK-POT**® slow cooker.

2. Combine teriyaki marinade, juice concentrate, water, marmalade and chile sauce in medium bowl; stir to blend. Pour over chicken. Cover; cook on LOW 3 to 3½ hours. Serve with rice.

Makes 8 to 9 servings

Spicy Orange
Chicken Nuggets

Spicy Asian Pork Bundles

1 boneless pork sirloin roast
(about 3 pounds)*

½ cup soy sauce

1 tablespoon chili garlic sauce
or chili paste

2 teaspoons minced fresh
ginger

2 tablespoons water

1 tablespoon cornstarch

2 teaspoons dark sesame oil

1 cup shredded carrots

10 large lettuce leaves

*Unless you have a 5-, 6- or 7-quart
CROCK-POT® slow cooker, cut any roast
larger than 2½ pounds in half so it cooks
completely.

1. Combine pork, soy sauce, chili garlic sauce and ginger in
CROCK-POT® slow cooker; mix well. Cover; cook on LOW 8 to
10 hours.

2. Remove roast to large cutting board; shred with two forks. Let
cooking liquid stand 5 minutes to allow fat to rise. Skim off and
discard fat.

3. Stir water, cornstarch and oil in small bowl until smooth; whisk
into cooking liquid. Turn **CROCK-POT**® slow cooker to HIGH. Cook,
uncovered, on HIGH 10 minutes or until sauce is thickened.

4. Stir in shredded pork and carrots. Cover; cook on HIGH 15 to
30 minutes or until heated through. Place ¼ cup pork filling into
lettuce leaves. Wrap to enclose.

Makes 10 bundles

Mu Shu Pork Bundles: Lightly spread prepared plum sauce over
small warm flour tortillas. Spoon ¼ cup pork filling and ¼ cup stir-fried
vegetables into flour tortillas. Wrap to enclose. Serve immediately. Makes
about 20 wraps.

Spicy Asian Pork Bundles

Asian Ginger Chicken Wings

3 pounds chicken wings, tips removed and split at joints

1 cup chopped red onion

1 cup soy sauce

¾ cup packed brown sugar

¼ cup dry sherry

2 tablespoons chopped fresh ginger

2 cloves garlic, minced

Chopped fresh chives

1. Preheat broiler. Broil chicken about 5 minutes per side. Remove to **CROCK-POT**® slow cooker.

2. Combine onion, soy sauce, brown sugar, sherry, ginger and garlic in medium bowl; stir to blend. Add to **CROCK-POT**® slow cooker; stir to coat. Cover; cook on LOW 5 to 6 hours or on HIGH 2 to 3 hours. Sprinkle with chives.

Makes 6 to 8 servings

Tip: You can also leave the wings whole and place them directly into the **CROCK-POT**® slow cooker. Removal of the tips and separating the double-boned piece from the drummette is optional.

Asian Ginger Chicken Wings

Curried Butternut Squash Soup

2 pounds butternut squash, rinsed, peeled, cored and chopped into 1-inch cubes

1 apple, peeled, cored and chopped

1 medium onion, chopped

5 cups chicken broth

1 tablespoon curry powder

¼ teaspoon ground cloves

Salt and black pepper

¼ cup chopped dried cranberries (optional)

1. Place squash, apple and onion in **CROCK-POT**® slow cooker.

2. Combine broth, curry powder and cloves in small bowl; stir to blend. Pour mixture into **CROCK-POT**® slow cooker. Cover; cook on LOW 5 to 5½ hours or on HIGH 4 hours.

3. Place soup in batches in food processor or blender; process to desired consistency. Season with salt and pepper. Garnish with cranberries.

Makes 8 servings

Curried Butternut Squash Soup

Hot and Sour Chicken

4 to 6 boneless, skinless
chicken breasts (1 to
1½ pounds total)

1 cup chicken broth

1 package (about 1 ounce)
dry hot-and-sour soup mix

Sugar snap peas and
chopped red bell pepper
(optional)

Place chicken in **CROCK-POT**® slow cooker; add broth and dry soup mix. Cover; cook on LOW 5 to 6 hours. Serve over peas and bell peppers, if desired.

Makes 4 to 6 servings

Tip: Here are a few simple steps to follow if you decide to debone your own chicken breasts.

1. For easier handling, freeze the chicken until it is firm, but not hard. Then remove the skin.

2. For each breast half, use a sharp knife to make three or four arched cuts between the meat and the bone, lifting the meat away with your free hand. (Or, slip your fingers between the meat and the bone. Then work the meat free without the aid of a knife.)

3. When the meat and bone are separated, remove the heavy white tendon that runs along the length of the breast. This will prevent the meat from shrinking as it cooks.

Hot and Sour Chicken

Sweet-Sour Cabbage
with Apples and Caraway Seeds

4 cups shredded red cabbage

1 large tart apple, peeled, cored and cut crosswise into ¼-inch-thick slices

¼ cup packed light brown sugar

¼ cup water

¼ cup cider vinegar

½ teaspoon salt

¼ teaspoon caraway seeds

Dash black pepper

Combine cabbage, apple, brown sugar, water, vinegar, salt, caraway seeds and pepper in **CROCK-POT**® slow cooker; stir to blend. Cover; cook on LOW 2½ to 3 hours.

Makes 6 servings

Chicken Congee

6 cups water

4 cups chicken broth

4 chicken drumsticks

1 cup uncooked white jasmine rice, rinsed and drained

1 (1-inch) piece ginger, sliced into 4 pieces

2 teaspoons kosher salt

¼ teaspoon ground white pepper

Optional toppings: soy sauce, sesame oil, thinly sliced green onions, fried shallots, fried garlic slices, salted roasted peanuts and/or pickled vegetables

1. Add water, broth, chicken, rice, ginger, salt and pepper to **CROCK-POT**® slow cooker. Cover; cook on LOW 8 hours or on HIGH 4 hours or until rice has completely broken down and mixture is thickened.

2. Remove and discard ginger. Remove chicken to large cutting board. Discard skin and bones. Shred chicken using two forks; stir back into **CROCK-POT**® slow cooker. Ladle congee into serving bowls; top with desired toppings.

Makes 6 servings

Sweet-Sour Cabbage with
Apples and Caraway Seeds

Sweet Gingered Spareribs

4 to 6 pounds pork spareribs,
cut into 1- or 2-rib pieces

Salt and black pepper

½ cup soy sauce

⅓ cup honey

¼ cup dry sherry

1 clove garlic, minced

¼ to ½ teaspoon ground ginger

2 tablespoons water

1 tablespoon cornstarch

1. Heat large skillet over medium-high heat. Season ribs with salt and pepper. Add ribs in batches; cook 3 to 5 minutes or until browned on both sides. Remove to **CROCK-POT**® slow cooker.

2. Combine soy sauce, honey, sherry, garlic and ginger in small bowl; pour over ribs. Cover; cook on LOW 6 to 8 hours.

3. Turn **CROCK-POT**® slow cooker to HIGH. Remove ribs to large serving plate. Stir water into cornstarch in small bowl until smooth; whisk into cooking liquid. Cook, uncovered, on HIGH 5 to 10 minutes or until sauce is thickened. Return ribs to sauce; stir to coat.

Makes 4 to 6 servings

Sweet Gingered Spareribs

Citrus Chinese Dates
with Toasted Hazelnuts

2 cups pitted dates

⅔ cup boiling water

½ cup sugar

    Strips of peel from 1 lemon
    (yellow part only)

Whipped cream (optional)

¼ cup hazelnuts, shelled and
    toasted*

*To toast hazelnuts, spread in single layer in
heavy skillet. Cook over medium heat 1 to
2 minutes or until nuts are lightly browned,
stirring frequently.*

1. Place dates in medium bowl; cover with water. Soak overnight to rehydrate. Drain; remove dates to **CROCK-POT**® slow cooker.

2. Add ⅔ cup boiling water, sugar and lemon peel to **CROCK-POT**® slow cooker. Cover; cook on HIGH 3 hours.

3. Remove and discard peel. Place dates in serving dishes. Top with whipped cream, if desired. Sprinkle with hazelnuts.

Makes 4 servings

Citrus Chinese Dates
with Toasted Hazelnuts

Asian Barbecue Skewers

2 pounds boneless, skinless chicken thighs

½ cup soy sauce

⅓ cup packed brown sugar

2 tablespoons sesame oil

3 cloves garlic, minced

1 tablespoon toasted sesame seeds (optional)*

To toast sesame seeds, spread in small skillet. Shake skillet over medium-low heat 2 minutes or until seeds begin to pop and turn golden brown.

1. Cut each chicken thigh into four pieces, about 1½ inches thick. Thread chicken onto 7-inch wooden skewers, folding thinner pieces, if necessary. Place skewers into **CROCK-POT**® slow cooker, layering as flat as possible.

2. Combine soy sauce, brown sugar, oil and garlic in small bowl. Reserve ⅓ cup sauce. Pour remaining sauce over skewers. Cover; cook on LOW 2 hours. Turn skewers over. Cover; cook on LOW 1 hour.

3. Remove skewers to large serving platter. Discard cooking liquid. Pour reserved sauce over skewers. Sprinkle with sesame seeds, if desired.

Makes 4 to 6 servings

ASIAN FLAVORS

Asian Barbecue Skewers

Pineapple and Pork Teriyaki

Nonstick cooking spray

2 pork tenderloins (1¼ pounds *each*)

1 can (8 ounces) pineapple chunks

½ cup teriyaki sauce

3 tablespoons honey

1 tablespoon minced fresh ginger

1. Spray large skillet with cooking spray; heat over medium-high heat. Add pork; cook 8 minutes or until browned on all sides. Remove to oval-shaped **CROCK-POT**® slow cooker.

2. Combine pineapple, teriyaki sauce, honey and ginger in large bowl; stir to blend. Pour over pork. Cover; cook on LOW 6 to 7 hours or on HIGH 3 to 4 hours. Remove to large cutting board; loosely tent with foil. Let stand 15 minutes before slicing.

3. Cover; cook on HIGH 10 to 15 minutes or until sauce is thickened. Serve sliced pork with pineapple and cooking liquid.

Makes 6 to 8 servings

Pineapple and Pork Teriyaki

ITALIAN CLASSICS

Manchego Eggplant

1 cup all-purpose flour

4 large eggplants, peeled and sliced horizontally into ¾-inch-thick pieces

2 tablespoons olive oil

1 jar (24 to 26 ounces) roasted garlic-flavor pasta sauce

2 tablespoons Italian seasoning

1 cup (4 ounces) grated manchego cheese

1 jar (24 to 26 ounces) roasted eggplant-flavor marinara pasta sauce

1. Place flour in medium shallow bowl. Add eggplant; toss to coat. Heat oil in large skillet over medium-high heat. Lightly brown eggplant in batches 3 to 4 minutes on each side.

2. Pour thin layer of garlic pasta sauce into bottom of **CROCK-POT**® slow cooker. Top with half of eggplant slices, Italian seasoning, cheese and marinara sauce. Repeat layers with remaining half of eggplant slices, Italian seasoning, cheese and marinara sauce. Cover; cook on HIGH 2 hours.

Makes 12 servings

Creamy Red Pepper Polenta

6 cups boiling water

2 cups yellow cornmeal

1 small red bell pepper, finely chopped

¼ cup (½ stick) butter, melted

2 teaspoons salt

¼ teaspoon paprika, plus additional for garnish

⅛ teaspoon ground red pepper

⅛ teaspoon ground cumin

Combine water, cornmeal, bell pepper, butter, salt, ¼ teaspoon paprika, ground red pepper and cumin in **CROCK-POT**® slow cooker; stir to blend. Cover; cook on LOW 3 to 4 hours or on HIGH 1 to 2 hours, stirring occasionally. Garnish with additional paprika.

Makes 4 to 6 servings

Creamy Red Pepper Polenta

Parmesan Potato Wedges

2 pounds red potatoes, cut
into ½-inch wedges

¼ cup finely chopped onion

1½ teaspoons dried oregano

½ teaspoon salt

¼ teaspoon black pepper

2 tablespoons butter, cubed

¼ cup grated Parmesan cheese

Layer potatoes, onion, oregano, salt and pepper in **CROCK-POT**®
slow cooker; dot with butter. Cover; cook on HIGH 4 hours. Remove
potatoes to large serving platter; sprinkle with cheese.

Makes 6 servings

Parmesan Potato Wedges

Pasta Shells with Prosciutto

3 cups (8 ounces) uncooked medium shell pasta

1 jar (24 to 26 ounces) vodka pasta sauce

¾ cup water

½ cup whipping cream

2 ounces (½ cup) torn or coarsely chopped thin sliced prosciutto

¼ cup chopped fresh chives

1. Coat inside of **CROCK-POT**® slow cooker with nonstick cooking spray. Combine pasta, pasta sauce and water in **CROCK-POT**® slow cooker. Cover; cook on LOW 2 hours or on HIGH 1 hour.

2. Stir in cream. Cover; cook on LOW 1 to 1½ hours or on HIGH 45 minutes to 1 hour or until pasta is tender.

3. Stir prosciutto into pasta mixture. Spoon into shallow bowls; top with chives.

Makes 4 servings

Pasta Shells
with Prosciutto

Italian Pot Roast with Mushrooms

6 slices bacon

1 boneless beef chuck roast
(2½ to 3 pounds), trimmed*

¾ teaspoon salt, divided

¼ teaspoon black pepper

¾ cup chopped shallots

8 ounces sliced white
mushrooms

4 cloves garlic, minced

1 tablespoon dried oregano

1 cup chicken broth

¼ cup tomato paste

Roasted Cauliflower (recipe
follows, optional)

*Unless you have a 5-, 6- or 7-quart
CROCK-POT* slow cooker, cut any roast
larger than 2½ pounds in half so it cooks
completely.*

1. Heat large skillet over medium heat. Add bacon; cook 7 to 8 minutes until crisp-cooked and tender. Remove to large paper towel-lined plate; crumble.

2. Pour off all but 2 tablespoons fat from skillet. Season roast with ½ teaspoon salt and pepper. Heat same skillet over medium-high heat. Add roast; cook 8 minutes or until well browned. Remove to large plate. Add shallots, mushrooms, garlic, oregano and remaining ¼ teaspoon salt; cook 3 to 4 minutes. Remove shallot mixture to **CROCK-POT**® slow cooker.

3. Stir bacon into **CROCK-POT**® slow cooker. Place roast on top of vegetables. Combine broth and tomato paste in small bowl; stir to blend. Pour broth mixture over roast. Cover; cook on LOW 8 hours. Remove roast to large cutting board. Let stand 10 minutes before slicing. Top with vegetables and cooking liquid.

Makes 6 to 8 servings

Roasted Cauliflower: Preheat oven to 375°F. Break cauliflower into florets; coat with olive oil. Roast 20 minutes. Turn, roast 15 minutes.

Turkey Italian Sausage with White Beans

1 pound turkey or pork Italian sausage, casings removed

½ cup minced onion

2 cans (about 15 ounces *each*) cannellini or Great Northern beans, rinsed and drained

1 can (about 14 ounces) Italian seasoned diced tomatoes

1 teaspoon dried rosemary

½ cup grated Parmesan or Romano cheese

1. Heat large skillet over medium-high heat. Brown sausage and onion 6 to 8 minutes, stirring to break up meat. Drain fat.

2. Coat inside of **CROCK-POT**® slow cooker with nonstick cooking spray. Combine beans, tomatoes and rosemary in **CROCK-POT**® slow cooker. Stir in sausage mixture. Cover; cook on LOW 3 to 4 hours or on HIGH 1½ to 2 hours. Ladle into bowls; top with cheese.

Makes 4 servings

Turkey Italian Sausage
with White Beans

Pesto Rice and Beans

1 can (about 15 ounces) Great Northern beans, rinsed and drained

1 can (about 14 ounces) chicken broth

¾ cup uncooked converted long grain rice

1½ cups frozen cut green beans, thawed and drained

½ cup prepared pesto

Fresh tomato, chopped (optional)

Grated Parmesan cheese (optional)

1. Combine Great Northern beans, broth and rice in **CROCK-POT**® slow cooker; stir to blend. Cover; cook on LOW 2 hours.

2. Stir green beans into **CROCK-POT**® slow cooker. Cover; cook on LOW 1 hour or until rice and beans are tender.

3. Turn off heat. Remove **CROCK-POT**® stoneware to heatproof surface. Stir in pesto. Let stand, covered, 5 minutes. Garnish with tomato and cheese.

Makes 8 servings

Tip: Choose converted long grain rice (or Arborio rice when suggested) or wild rice for best results. Long, slow cooking can turn other types of rice into mush; if you prefer to use another type of rice instead of converted rice, cook it on the stove-top and add it to the **CROCK-POT**® slow cooker during the last 15 minutes of cooking.

Pesto Rice and Beans

Cheesy Polenta

6 cups vegetable broth

1½ cups uncooked medium-grind instant polenta

½ cup grated Parmesan cheese, plus additional for serving

4 tablespoons unsalted butter, cubed

1. Coat inside of **CROCK-POT®** slow cooker with nonstick cooking spray. Heat broth in large saucepan over high heat. Remove to **CROCK-POT®** slow cooker; whisk in polenta.

2. Cover; cook on LOW 2 to 2½ hours or until polenta is tender and creamy. Stir in ½ cup cheese and butter. Serve with additional cheese.

Makes 6 servings

Tip: Spread any leftover polenta in a baking dish and refrigerate until cold. Cut cold polenta into sticks or slices. You can then fry or grill the polenta until lightly browned.

Cheesy Polenta

Beefy Tortellini

½ pound ground beef or turkey

1 jar (24 to 26 ounces) roasted tomato and garlic pasta sauce

1 package (12 ounces) uncooked three-cheese tortellini

8 ounces sliced button or exotic mushrooms, such as oyster, shiitake and cremini

½ cup water

½ teaspoon red pepper flakes (optional)

¾ cup grated Asiago or Romano cheese

Chopped fresh Italian parsley (optional)

1. Coat inside of **CROCK-POT**® slow cooker with nonstick cooking spray. Brown beef in large skillet over medium-high heat 6 to 8 minutes, stirring to break up meat. Remove to **CROCK-POT**® slow cooker using slotted spoon.

2. Stir in pasta sauce, tortellini, mushrooms, water and red pepper flakes, if desired. Cover; cook on LOW 2 hours or on HIGH 1 hour. Stir.

3. Cover; cook on LOW 2 to 2½ hours or on HIGH ½ to 1 hour. Serve in shallow bowls topped with cheese and parsley, if desired.

Makes 6 servings

Beefy Tortellini

Italian Beef

1 boneless beef rump roast
   (3 to 5 pounds)*

1 can (about 14 ounces) beef
   broth

2 cups mild giardiniera

8 crusty Italian bread rolls,
   split

*Unless you have a 5-, 6- or 7-quart
CROCK-POT® *slow cooker, cut any roast
larger than 2½ pounds in half so it cooks
completely.*

1. Place beef in **CROCK-POT**® slow cooker; add broth and giardiniera.
Cover; cook on LOW 10 hours.

2. Remove beef to large cutting board; shred with two forks. Return
beef to cooking liquid; stir to blend. To serve, spoon beef and sauce
onto rolls.

Makes 8 servings

Italian Beef

Macaroni and Cheese

6 cups cooked elbow macaroni

2 tablespoons butter

6 cups (24 ounces) shredded
Cheddar cheese

4 cups evaporated milk

2 teaspoons salt

½ teaspoon black pepper

Toss macaroni with butter in large bowl. Stir in cheese, evaporated milk, salt and pepper. Remove to **CROCK-POT**® slow cooker. Cover; cook on HIGH 2 to 3 hours.

Makes 6 to 8 servings

Tip: Make this mac and cheese recipe more fun by adding some tasty mix-ins. Diced green or red bell pepper, peas, hot dog slices, chopped tomato, browned ground beef or chopped onion are all great options. Be creative!

Macaroni and Cheese

Rigatoni with Broccoli Rabe and Sausage

2 tablespoons olive oil

3 sweet or hot Italian sausage
links, casings removed

2 cloves garlic, minced

1 large bunch (about
1¼ pounds) broccoli rabe

½ cup chicken broth

½ teaspoon red pepper flakes

1 pound uncooked rigatoni

Grated Parmesan cheese
(optional)

1. Coat inside of **CROCK-POT**® slow cooker with nonstick cooking spray.

2. Heat oil in large skillet over medium heat. Add sausage; cook and stir 6 to 8 minutes, stirring to break up meat. Drain fat. Add garlic; cook and stir 1 minute or until softened and fragrant. Remove to **CROCK-POT**® slow cooker.

3. Trim any stiff, woody parts from bottoms of broccoli rabe stems; discard. Cut broccoli rabe into 1-inch lengths. Place in large bowl of cold water; stir with hands to wash well. Lift broccoli rabe out of water by handfuls leaving any sand or dirt in bottom of bowl. Shake well to remove excess water, but do not dry. Add to **CROCK-POT**® slow cooker with sausage. Add broth and red pepper flakes. Cover; cook on LOW 4 hours or on HIGH 2 hours.

4. Meanwhile, cook rigatoni according to package directions. Stir into sausage mixture just before serving. Garnish with cheese.

Makes 6 servings

Rigatoni with Broccoli Rabe and Sausage

Garlic and Herb Polenta

3 tablespoons butter, divided

8 cups water

2 cups yellow cornmeal

2 teaspoons finely minced
   garlic

2 teaspoons salt

3 tablespoons chopped fresh
   herbs such as Italian
   parsley, chives, thyme or
   chervil (or a combination)

Coat inside of **CROCK-POT**® slow cooker with 1 tablespoon butter. Stir in water, cornmeal, garlic, salt and remaining 2 tablespoons butter. Cover; cook on LOW 4 hours or on HIGH 3 hours, stirring occasionally. Stir in chopped herbs just before serving.

Makes 6 servings

Garlic and Herb Polenta

Chicken Scaloppine in Alfredo Sauce

2 tablespoons all-purpose flour

¼ teaspoon salt

¼ teaspoon black pepper

6 boneless, skinless chicken tenderloins (about 1 pound), cut lengthwise in half

1 tablespoon butter

1 tablespoon olive oil

1 cup Alfredo pasta sauce

1 package (12 ounces) uncooked spinach noodles

1. Place flour, salt and pepper in large bowl; stir to combine. Add chicken; toss to coat. Heat butter and oil in large skillet over medium-high heat. Add chicken; cook 3 minutes per side or until browned. Remove chicken in single layer to **CROCK-POT**® slow cooker.

2. Add Alfredo pasta sauce to **CROCK-POT**® slow cooker. Cover; cook on LOW 1 to 1½ hours.

3. Meanwhile, cook noodles according to package directions. Drain; place in large shallow bowl. Spoon chicken and sauce over noodles.

Makes 6 servings

Chicken Scaloppine
in Alfredo Sauce

Bagna Cauda

¾ cup olive oil

6 tablespoons butter, softened

12 anchovy fillets, drained

6 cloves garlic

⅛ teaspoon red pepper flakes

Optional dippers: endive spears, cauliflower florets, cucumber spears, carrot sticks, zucchini spears, red bell pepper pieces, sugar snap peas and/or crusty bread slices

Place oil, butter, anchovies, garlic and red pepper flakes in food processor; process until smooth. Pour into 2½-quart or other small-sized **CROCK-POT**® slow cooker. Cover; cook on LOW 2 hours or until heated through. Serve with desired dippers.

Makes 10 to 12 servings

Tip: Bagna cauda is a warm Italian dip similar to the more famous fondue. The name is derived from "bagno caldo," meaning "warm bath" in Italian. This dip should be kept warm while serving, just like you would fondue.

Bagna Cauda

MEXICAN FIESTA

Simple Shredded Pork Tacos

2 pounds boneless pork roast

1 cup salsa

1 can (4 ounces) chopped mild green chiles

½ teaspoon garlic salt

½ teaspoon black pepper

Corn or flour tortillas

Optional toppings: salsa, sour cream, jalapeño pepper slices, diced tomatoes, shredded cheese and/or shredded lettuce

1. Place roast, 1 cup salsa, chiles, garlic salt and black pepper in **CROCK-POT**® slow cooker. Cover; cook on LOW 8 hours.

2. Remove pork to large cutting board; shred with two forks. Serve on tortillas with sauce and desired toppings.

Makes 6 servings

Tip: To warm tortillas, stack 6 to 8 tortillas and wrap them in plastic wrap. Microwave at HIGH about 40 to 50 seconds, turning over and rotating ¼ turn once during heating. For 1 or 2 tortillas, wrap and heat at HIGH about 20 seconds.

Chipotle Chili con Queso Dip

10 ounces pasteurized process
    cheese product, cubed

¼ cup mild chunky salsa

½ canned chipotle pepper
    in adobo sauce, finely
    chopped*

½ teaspoon Worcestershire
    sauce

⅛ teaspoon chili powder

Pretzels

Use more to taste.

1. Coat inside of **CROCK-POT**® slow cooker with nonstick cooking spray. Add cheese product, salsa, chipotle pepper, Worcestershire sauce and chili powder; stir to blend. Cover; cook on LOW 1 hour.

2. Stir well. Cover; cook on LOW 30 minutes or until cheese is melted. Stir until smooth. Serve with pretzels.

Makes 1½ cups

Chipotle Chili con Queso Dip

Easy Family Burritos

1 boneless beef chuck
   shoulder roast (2 to
   3 pounds)*

1 jar (24 ounces) *or* 2 jars
   (16 ounces *each*) salsa

Flour tortillas, warmed

Optional toppings: shredded
   cheese, sour cream, salsa,
   shredded lettuce, diced
   tomato, diced onion and/
   or guacamole

**Unless you have a 5-, 6- or 7-quart
CROCK-POT® slow cooker, cut any roast
larger than 2½ pounds in half so it cooks
completely.*

1. Place beef in **CROCK-POT®** slow cooker; top with salsa. Cover; cook on LOW 8 to 10 hours.

2. Remove beef to large cutting board; shred with two forks. Return to cooking liquid; stir to blend. Cover; cook on LOW 30 minutes or until heated through. Serve in tortillas. Top as desired.

Makes 8 servings

Easy Family Burritos

Salsa-Style Wings

2 tablespoons vegetable oil

1½ pounds chicken wings
(about 18 wings)

2 cups salsa

¼ cup packed brown sugar

Sprigs fresh cilantro
(optional)

1. Heat oil in large skillet over medium-high heat. Add wings in batches; cook 3 to 4 minutes or until browned on all sides. Remove to **CROCK-POT**® slow cooker.

2. Combine salsa and brown sugar in medium bowl; stir to blend. Pour over wings. Cover; cook on LOW 5 to 6 hours or on HIGH 2 to 3 hours. Serve with salsa mixture. Garnish with cilantro.

Makes 4 servings

Salsa-Style Wings

Refried Bean Dip with Blue Tortilla Chips

3 cans (about 16 ounces *each*) refried beans

1 cup prepared taco sauce

½ teaspoon salt

½ teaspoon black pepper

3 cups (12 ounces) shredded Cheddar cheese

¾ cup chopped green onions

2 packages (12 ounces *each*) blue tortilla chips

Combine refried beans, taco sauce, salt and pepper in large bowl; stir to blend. Spread one third of bean mixture on bottom of **CROCK-POT**® slow cooker. Sprinkle evenly with ¾ cup cheese. Repeat layers two times, finishing with cheese layer. Sprinkle green onions evenly on cheese. Cover; cook on LOW 2 to 4 hours. Serve with tortilla chips.

Makes 10 servings

Refried Bean Dip with Blue Tortilla Chips

Super-Easy Beef Burritos

1 boneless beef chuck roast
   (2 to 3 pounds)*

1 can (28 ounces) enchilada
   sauce

2 to 3 tablespoons water
   (optional)

4 (8-inch) flour tortillas

*Unless you have a 5-, 6- or 7-quart
CROCK-POT® slow cooker, cut any roast
larger than 2½ pounds in half so it cooks
completely.*

Place roast in **CROCK-POT®** slow cooker; cover with enchilada sauce. Add water, if desired. Cover; cook on LOW 6 to 8 hours. Remove beef to large cutting board; shred with two forks. Serve in tortillas.

Makes 4 servings

Serving Suggestion: Excellent garnishes include shredded cheese, sour cream, salsa, lettuce and tomatoes.

Super-Easy Beef Burritos

Carne Rellenos

1 can (4 ounces) whole mild
  green chiles, drained

4 ounces cream cheese,
  softened

1 flank steak (about 2 pounds)

1½ cups salsa verde

Hot cooked rice (optional)

1. Slit green chiles open on one side with sharp knife; stuff with cream cheese.

2. Open steak flat on sheet of waxed paper. Score steak; turn over. Lay stuffed chiles across unscored side of steak. Roll up; tie with kitchen string.

3. Place steak in **CROCK-POT**® slow cooker; pour in salsa. Cover; cook on LOW 6 to 8 hours or on HIGH 3 to 4 hours. Remove steak to large cutting board. Let stand 10 to 15 minutes before slicing. Serve over rice, if desired, with cooking liquid.

Makes 6 servings

Carne Rellenos

Chili Verde

1 tablespoon vegetable oil

1 to 2 pounds boneless pork chops

2 cups sliced carrots

1 jar (24 ounces) mild green salsa

1 cup chopped onion

1. Heat oil in large skillet over medium-low heat. Add pork; cook 3 to 5 minutes or until browned on both sides.

2. Place carrots in bottom of **CROCK-POT**® slow cooker; top with pork. Pour salsa and onion over pork. Cover; cook on HIGH 6 to 8 hours.

Makes 4 to 8 servings

Serving Suggestion: The pork can also be shredded and served in tortillas.

Chili Verde

Shredded Pork Wraps

1 cup salsa, divided

2 tablespoons cornstarch

1 boneless pork sirloin roast
(2 pounds)

6 (8-inch) flour tortillas

3 cups broccoli slaw mix

½ cup (2 ounces) shredded
Cheddar cheese

1. Stir ¼ cup salsa into cornstarch in small bowl until smooth. Pour cornstarch mixture into **CROCK-POT**® slow cooker. Top with pork. Pour remaining ¾ cup salsa over pork. Cover; cook on LOW 6 to 8 hours.

2. Remove pork to large cutting board; shred with two forks. Divide shredded meat evenly among tortillas. Spoon about 2 tablespoons salsa mixture on top of meat in each tortilla. Top evenly with broccoli slaw and cheese. Fold bottom edge of tortilla over filling; fold in sides. Roll up completely to enclose filling. Serve remaining salsa mixture as dipping sauce.

Makes 6 servings

Shredded Pork Wraps

Mexican-Style Spinach

3 packages (10 ounces *each*)
   frozen chopped spinach,
   thawed

1 tablespoon canola oil

1 onion, chopped

1 clove garlic, minced

2 Anaheim chiles, roasted,
   peeled and minced*

3 fresh tomatillos, roasted,
   husks removed and
   chopped**

*To roast chiles, heat large heavy skillet over medium-high heat. Add chiles; cook and turn until blackened all over. Place chiles in brown paper bag 2 to 5 minutes. Remove chiles from bag; scrape off charred skin. Cut off top and pull out core. Slice lengthwise; scrape off veins and any remaining seeds with a knife.

**To roast tomatillos, heat large heavy skillet over medium heat. Add tomatillos with papery husks; cook 10 minutes or until husks are brown and interior flesh is soft. Remove and discard husks when cool enough to handle.

1. Place spinach in **CROCK-POT**® slow cooker.

2. Heat oil in large skillet over medium heat. Add onion and garlic; cook and stir 5 minutes or until onion is tender. Add chiles and tomatillos; cook 3 to 4 minutes. Remove onion mixture to **CROCK-POT**® slow cooker. Cover; cook on LOW 4 to 6 hours.

Makes 6 servings

Mexican-Style Spinach

Posole

3 pounds boneless pork, cubed

2 cans (about 15 ounces *each*) white hominy, drained

1 package (10 ounces) frozen white corn, thawed

¾ cup chili sauce

Combine pork, hominy, corn and chili sauce in **CROCK-POT®** slow cooker; stir to blend. Cover; cook on LOW 10 hours or on HIGH 5 hours.

Makes 8 servings

Posole

Fiesta Dip

8 ounces canned refried beans

½ cup (2 ounces) shredded Cheddar cheese, plus additional for garnish

⅓ cup chopped green chile pepper*

¼ cup salsa

Tortilla or corn chips

Chopped fresh tomatoes

Chile peppers can sting and irritate the skin, so wear rubber gloves when handling peppers and do not touch your eyes.

Coat inside of **CROCK-POT**® slow cooker with nonstick cooking spray. Combine beans, ½ cup cheese, chile pepper and salsa in **CROCK-POT**® slow cooker. Cover; cook on LOW 45 minutes or until cheese is melted, stirring occasionally. Serve on tortilla chips. Garnish with tomatoes and additional cheese.

Makes 16 servings

Fiesta Dip

Shredded Chicken Tacos

2 pounds boneless, skinless
    chicken thighs
½ cup prepared mango salsa,
    plus additional for serving

Shredded lettuce (optional)
8 (6-inch) corn tortillas,
    warmed

1. Coat inside of **CROCK-POT**® slow cooker with nonstick cooking spray. Add chicken and ½ cup salsa. Cover; cook on LOW 4 to 5 hours or on HIGH 2½ to 3 hours.

2. Remove chicken to large cutting board; shred with two forks. Stir shredded chicken back into **CROCK-POT**® slow cooker. To serve, divide chicken and lettuce, if desired, evenly among tortillas. Serve with additional salsa.

Makes 4 servings

Shredded Chicken Tacos

Chorizo Chili

1 pound ground beef

8 ounces bulk raw chorizo sausage *or* ½ (15-ounce) package raw chorizo sausage, casings removed*

1 can (about 15 ounces) chili beans in chili sauce

2 cans (about 14 ounces *each*) chili-style diced tomatoes

Optional toppings: sour cream, chopped fresh chives and/or shredded Cheddar cheese

A highly seasoned Mexican pork sausage.

1. Brown beef and chorizo in large skillet over medium-high heat 6 to 8 minutes, stirring to break up meat. Remove beef mixture to **CROCK-POT**® slow cooker using slotted spoon. Stir beans and tomatoes into **CROCK-POT**® slow cooker.

2. Cover; cook on LOW 7 hours. Turn off heat. Let stand 10 to 12 minutes. Skim off and discard fat. Top as desired.

Makes 6 servings

Chorizo Chili

Mexican Meat Loaf

2 pounds ground beef

2 cups crushed corn chips

1 cup (4 ounces) shredded
    Cheddar cheese

⅔ cup salsa

2 eggs, beaten

¼ cup taco seasoning

Combine beef, chips, cheese, salsa, eggs and taco seasoning in large bowl; mix well. Shape meat mixture into loaf and place in **CROCK-POT**® slow cooker. Cover; cook on LOW 8 to 10 hours.

Makes 4 to 6 servings

Tip: To glaze meat loaf, mix together ½ cup ketchup, 2 tablespoons packed brown sugar and 1 teaspoon dry mustard. Spread over the cooked meat loaf. Turn **CROCK-POT**® slow cooker to HIGH. Cover; cook on HIGH 15 minutes.

Mexican Meat Loaf

Mile-High Enchilada Pie

5 (6-inch) corn tortillas

1 jar (12 ounces) salsa

1 can (about 15 ounces) kidney beans, rinsed and drained

1 cup shredded cooked chicken

1 cup (4 ounces) shredded Monterey Jack cheese with jalapeño peppers

Chopped fresh cilantro and sliced red bell pepper (optional)

1. Prepare foil handles by tearing off three 18×2-inch strips heavy foil (or use regular foil folded to double thickness). Crisscross foil strips in spoke design; place in **CROCK-POT**® slow cooker to make lifting tortilla stack easier. Place 1 tortilla on top of foil handles. Top with small amount of salsa, beans, chicken and cheese. Continue layering in order using remaining ingredients, ending with tortilla and cheese. Cover; cook on LOW 6 to 8 hours or on HIGH 3 to 4 hours.

2. Pull pie out by foil handles. Garnish with fresh cilantro and sliced red bell pepper.

Makes 4 to 6 servings

Mile-High Enchilada Pie

Chicken and Spicy Black Bean Tacos

1 can (about 15 ounces) black beans, rinsed and drained

1 can (10 ounces) diced tomatoes with mild green chiles, drained

1½ teaspoons chili powder

¾ teaspoon ground cumin

1 tablespoon plus 1 teaspoon extra virgin olive oil, divided

12 ounces boneless, skinless chicken breasts

12 crisp corn taco shells

Optional toppings: shredded lettuce, diced tomatoes, shredded Cheddar cheese, sour cream and/or sliced black olives

1. Coat inside of **CROCK-POT®** slow cooker with nonstick cooking spray. Add beans and tomatoes with chiles. Combine chili powder, cumin and 1 teaspoon oil in small bowl; rub onto chicken. Place chicken in **CROCK-POT®** slow cooker. Cover; cook on HIGH 1¾ hours.

2. Remove chicken to large cutting board; slice. Remove bean mixture to large bowl using slotted spoon. Stir in remaining 1 tablespoon oil.

3. To serve, warm taco shells according to package directions. Fill with equal amounts of bean mixture and chicken. Top as desired.

Makes 4 servings

Chicken and Spicy
Black Bean Tacos

Mexican Chicken

2 to 4 boneless, skinless
chicken breasts

1 medium onion, sliced

1 can (10¾ ounces) condensed
cream of chicken soup,
undiluted

1 can (10 ounces) Mexican-
style diced tomatoes with
mild green chiles

1 package (8 ounces)
pasteurized process
cheese product, cubed

Hot cooked spaghetti

1. Place chicken, onion, soup and tomatoes with chiles in **CROCK-POT**®
slow cooker. Cover; cook on LOW 6 to 8 hours or on HIGH 4 hours.

2. Break up chicken into pieces. Add cheese product. Cover; cook
on HIGH 10 minutes or until cheese product is melted. Serve over
spaghetti.

Makes 2 to 4 servings

Mexican Chicken

Dulce de Leche

1 can (14 ounces) sweetened
    condensed milk

Pour milk into 9×5-inch loaf pan; cover tightly with foil. Place loaf pan in **CROCK-POT**® slow cooker. Pour enough water to reach halfway up sides of loaf pan. Cover; cook on LOW 5 to 6 hours or until golden and thickened.

Serving Suggestion: Try this Dulce de Leche as a fondue with bananas, apples, shortbread, chocolate wafers, pretzels and/or waffle cookies.

Dulce de Leche

Spicy Shredded Chicken

6 boneless, skinless chicken breasts (about 1½ pounds)

1 jar (16 ounces) salsa

Flour tortillas, warmed

Optional toppings: shredded cheese, sour cream, shredded lettuce, diced tomato, diced onion and/ or sliced avocado

1. Place chicken in **CROCK-POT**® slow cooker; top with salsa. Cover; cook on LOW 6 to 8 hours.

2. Remove chicken to large cutting board; shred with two forks. Serve in tortillas. Top as desired.

Makes 6 servings

Shredded Beef Wraps

1 beef flank steak or beef skirt steak (1 to 1½ pounds)

1 cup beef broth

½ cup sun-dried tomatoes (not packed in oil), chopped

3 to 4 cloves garlic, minced

¼ teaspoon ground cumin

4 (8-inch) flour tortillas

Shredded lettuce, diced tomatoes and shredded Monterey Jack cheese (optional)

1. Cut flank steak into quarters. Place flank steak, broth, sun-dried tomatoes, garlic and cumin in **CROCK-POT**® slow cooker. Cover; cook on LOW 7 to 8 hours.

2. Remove steak to large cutting board; shred with two forks. Place remaining juices from **CROCK-POT**® slow cooker in blender or food processor; blend until sauce is smooth.

3. Spoon steak onto tortillas with small amount of sauce. Garnish with lettuce, diced tomatoes and cheese.

Makes 4 servings

Spicy Shredded Chicken

VEGETARIAN FAVORITES

Olive Oil Mashed Rutabagas

1 (2½ to 3-pound) rutabaga
(waxed turnip), peeled and
cut into 1-inch pieces

4 cloves garlic

Boiling water

2 tablespoons olive oil

1 teaspoon dried thyme

1 teaspoon salt

1. Combine rutabaga, garlic and enough boiling water to cover by 1 inch in **CROCK-POT®** slow cooker. Cover; cook on LOW 7 to 8 hours.

2. Place rutabaga in food processor or blender; purée, adding water as necessary to reach desired consistency. Stir in oil, salt and thyme.

Makes 8 servings

Beans and Spinach Bruschetta

2 cans (about 15 ounces *each*) Great Northern or cannellini beans

3 cloves garlic, minced

Salt and black pepper

3 tablespoons extra virgin olive oil, divided

6 cups spinach, loosely packed and finely chopped

1 tablespoon red wine vinegar

16 slices whole grain baguette

1. Combine beans, garlic, salt and black pepper in **CROCK-POT**® slow cooker; stir to blend. Cover; cook on LOW 3 hours or until beans are tender. Turn off heat. Mash beans with potato masher.

2. Heat 1 tablespoon oil in large skillet over medium heat. Add spinach; cook 2 to 3 minutes or until wilted. Stir in vinegar, salt and pepper. Remove from heat.

3. Preheat grill or broiler. Brush baguette slices with remaining 2 tablespoons oil. Grill 5 to 7 minutes or until bread is golden brown and crisp. Top with bean mixture and spinach.

Makes 16 servings

Spiced Sweet Potatoes

2 pounds sweet potatoes, peeled and cut into ½-inch pieces

¼ cup packed dark brown sugar

1 teaspoon ground cinnamon

½ teaspoon ground nutmeg

⅛ teaspoon salt

2 tablespoons unsalted butter, cut into small pieces

1 teaspoon vanilla

Combine potatoes, brown sugar, cinnamon, nutmeg and salt in **CROCK-POT**® slow cooker; mix well. Cover; cook on LOW 7 hours or on HIGH 4 hours. Stir in butter and vanilla.

Makes 4 servings

Beans and Spinach Bruschetta

Spanish Paella-Style Rice

2 cans (about 14 ounces *each*) vegetable broth

1½ cups uncooked converted long grain rice

1 small red bell pepper, chopped

⅓ cup dry white wine or water

½ teaspoon saffron threads, crushed or ½ teaspoon ground turmeric

⅛ teaspoon red pepper flakes

½ cup frozen peas, thawed

Salt

1. Combine broth, rice, bell pepper, wine, saffron and red pepper flakes in **CROCK-POT®** slow cooker; stir to blend. Cover; cook on LOW 4 hours or until liquid is absorbed.

2. Stir in peas. Turn **CROCK-POT®** slow cooker to HIGH. Cover; cook on HIGH 15 to 30 minutes or until peas are heated through. Season with salt.

Makes 6 servings

Cheesy Slow Cooker Potatoes

1 bag (32 ounces) shredded hash brown potatoes

2 cans (10½ ounces *each*) condensed Cheddar cheese soup, undiluted

1 can (12 ounces) evaporated milk

1 cup chopped onion

Combine potatoes, soup, evaporated milk and onion in **CROCK-POT®** slow cooker. Cover; cook on LOW 6 to 8 hours.

Makes 6 servings

Orange-Spiced Glazed Carrots

1 package (32 ounces) baby
    carrots

1/4 cup packed light brown
    sugar

1/2 cup orange juice

1 tablespoon butter

3/4 teaspoon ground cinnamon

1/4 teaspoon ground nutmeg

1/4 cup cold water

2 tablespoons cornstarch

1. Combine carrots, brown sugar, orange juice, butter, cinnamon
and nutmeg in **CROCK-POT**® slow cooker; stir to blend. Cover; cook
on LOW 3½ to 4 hours. Remove carrots to large serving bowl using
slotted spoon.

2. Turn **CROCK-POT**® slow cooker to HIGH. Stir water into cornstarch
in small bowl until smooth; whisk into cooking liquid. Cover; cook on
HIGH 15 minutes or until thickened. Spoon sauce over carrots.

Makes 6 servings

Chili and Cheese "Baked" Potato Supper

4 russet potatoes (about
    2 pounds), unpeeled

2 cups prepared meatless chili

1/2 cup (2 ounces) shredded
    Cheddar cheese

1/4 cup sour cream

2 green onions, sliced

1. Prick potatoes in several places with fork. Wrap potatoes in foil.
Place in **CROCK-POT**® slow cooker. Cover; cook on LOW 8 to 10 hours
or on HIGH 4 to 5 hours.

2. Carefully unwrap potatoes and place on serving dish. Place chili in
medium microwavable dish; microwave at HIGH 3 to 5 minutes. Split
potatoes and spoon chili on top. Sprinkle with cheese, sour cream
and green onions.

Makes 4 servings

Orange-Spiced
Glazed Carrots

Spinach Gorgonzola Corn Bread

2 boxes (8½ ounces *each*)
   corn bread mix

1 box (10 ounces) frozen
   chopped spinach, thawed
   and drained

1 cup crumbled Gorgonzola
   cheese

3 eggs

½ cup whipping cream

1 teaspoon black pepper

Paprika (optional)

1. Coat inside of 5-quart **CROCK-POT**® slow cooker with nonstick cooking spray. Combine corn bread mix, spinach, cheese, eggs, cream, pepper and paprika, if desired, in medium bowl; stir to blend. Pour batter into **CROCK-POT**® slow cooker. Cover; cook on HIGH 1½ hours.

2. Turn off heat. Let bread cool completely before inverting onto large serving platter.

Makes 1 loaf

Note: Cook only on HIGH setting for proper crust and texture.

Cauliflower Mash

2 heads cauliflower
   (8 cups florets)

1 tablespoon butter

1 tablespoon milk

Salt

Sprigs fresh Italian parsley
   (optional)

1. Arrange cauliflower in **CROCK-POT**® slow cooker. Add enough water to fill **CROCK-POT**® slow cooker by about 2 inches. Cover; cook on LOW 5 to 6 hours. Drain well.

2. Place cooked cauliflower in food processor or blender; process until almost smooth. Add butter; process until smooth. Add milk as needed to reach desired consistency. Season with salt. Garnish with parsley.

Makes 6 servings

Spinach Gorgonzola
Corn Bread

Cheesy Broccoli Casserole

2 packages (10 ounces *each*) frozen chopped broccoli

1 can (10½ ounces) condensed cream of celery soup, undiluted

1¼ cups (5 ounces) shredded sharp Cheddar cheese, divided

¼ cup minced onion

1 teaspoon paprika

1 teaspoon hot pepper sauce

½ teaspoon celery seed

1 cup crushed potato chips or saltine crackers

1. Coat inside of **CROCK-POT**® slow cooker with nonstick cooking spray. Combine broccoli, soup, 1 cup cheese, onion, paprika, hot pepper sauce and celery seed in **CROCK-POT**® slow cooker; stir to blend. Cover; cook on LOW 5 to 6 hours or on HIGH 2½ to 3 hours.

2. Uncover; sprinkle top with potato chips and remaining ¼ cup cheese. Cook, uncovered, on HIGH 10 to 15 minutes or until cheese is melted.

Makes 4 to 6 servings

Variations: Substitute thawed chopped spinach for the broccoli and top with spicy croutons.

Candied Sweet Potatoes

3 medium sweet potatoes (1½ to 2 pounds), sliced into ½-inch rounds

½ cup water

¼ cup (½ stick) butter, cut into pieces

3 tablespoons sugar

1 tablespoon vanilla

1 teaspoon ground nutmeg

Combine sweet potatoes, water, butter, sugar, vanilla and nutmeg in **CROCK-POT**® slow cooker; stir to blend. Cover; cook on LOW 7 hours or on HIGH 4 hours.

Makes 4 servings

Cheesy Broccoli Casserole

Mediterranean Red Potatoes

3 medium unpeeled red
    potatoes, cubed

⅔ cup fresh or frozen pearl
    onions

Garlic-flavored cooking
    spray

¾ teaspoon Italian seasoning

¼ teaspoon black pepper

1 small tomato, seeded and
    chopped

2 ounces feta cheese,
    crumbled

2 tablespoons chopped black
    olives

1. Place potatoes and onions in 1½-quart soufflé dish that fits inside of **CROCK-POT**® slow cooker. Spray with garlic-flavored cooking spray; toss to coat. Add Italian seasoning and pepper; mix well. Cover dish tightly with foil.

2. Make foil handles using three 18×2-inch strips of heavy-duty foil or use regular foil folded to double thickness. Crisscross foil in spoke design; place across bottom and up side of stoneware. Place soufflé dish in center of strips in **CROCK-POT**® slow cooker. Pull foil strips up and over dish.

3. Pour hot water into **CROCK-POT**® slow cooker to about 1½ inches from top of soufflé dish. Cover; cook on LOW 7 to 8 hours.

4. Use foil handles to lift dish out of **CROCK-POT**® slow cooker. Stir tomato, cheese and olives into potato mixture.

Makes 4 servings

Mediterranean Red Potatoes

Collard Greens

4 bunches collard greens, stemmed, washed and torn into bite-size pieces

2 cups water

½ medium red bell pepper, cut into strips

⅓ medium green bell pepper, cut into strips

¼ cup olive oil

¼ teaspoon salt

¼ teaspoon black pepper

Combine collard greens, water, bell peppers, oil, salt and black pepper in **CROCK-POT**® slow cooker; stir to blend. Cover; cook on LOW 3 to 4 hours or on HIGH 2 hours.

Makes 10 servings

Cheese Soup

2 cans (10¾ ounces *each*) condensed cream of celery soup, undiluted

4 cups (16 ounces) shredded Cheddar cheese

1 teaspoon paprika, plus additional for garnish

1 teaspoon Worcestershire sauce

1¼ cups half-and-half

Salt and black pepper

Snipped fresh chives (optional)

1. Combine soup, cheese, 1 teaspoon paprika and Worcestershire sauce in **CROCK-POT**® slow cooker; stir to blend. Cover; cook on LOW 2 to 3 hours.

2. Add half-and-half; stir until blended. Cover; cook on LOW 20 minutes. Season to taste with salt and pepper. Sprinkle with additional paprika and chives.

Makes 4 servings

Tip: Turn simple soup into a super supper by serving it in individual bread bowls. Cut a small slice from the tops of small, round loaves of a hearty bread (such as Italian or sourdough) and remove the insides, leaving a 1½-inch shell. Pour in soup and serve.

Collard Greens

Simmered Napa Cabbage with Dried Apricots

4 cups napa cabbage or green cabbage, cored, cleaned and thinly sliced

1 cup chopped dried apricots

¼ cup clover honey

2 tablespoons orange juice

½ cup dry red wine

Salt and black pepper

Grated orange peel (optional)

1. Combine cabbage and apricots in **CROCK-POT**® slow cooker; toss to blend.

2. Combine honey and orange juice in small bowl; stir until smooth. Drizzle over cabbage. Add wine. Cover; cook on LOW 5 to 6 hours or on HIGH 2 to 3 hours.

3. Season with salt and pepper. Garnish with orange peel.

Makes 8 servings

Winter Squash and Apples

1 teaspoon salt, plus additional for seasoning

½ teaspoon black pepper, plus additional for seasoning

1 butternut squash (about 2 pounds)

2 apples, sliced

1 medium onion, quartered and sliced

1½ tablespoons butter

1. Combine 1 teaspoon salt and ½ teaspoon pepper in small bowl.

2. Cut squash into 2-inch pieces; place in **CROCK-POT**® slow cooker. Add apples and onion. Sprinkle with salt and pepper mixture; stir well. Cover; cook on LOW 6 to 7 hours or until vegetables are tender.

3. Stir in butter and season to taste with additional salt and pepper.

Makes 4 to 6 servings

Simmered Napa Cabbage
with Dried Apricots

Slow-Good Apples and Carrots

6 carrots, sliced into ½-inch slices

4 apples, peeled, cored and sliced

¼ cup plus 1 tablespoon all-purpose flour

1 tablespoon packed brown sugar

½ teaspoon ground nutmeg

1 tablespoon butter, cubed

½ cup orange juice

Layer carrots and apples in **CROCK-POT®** slow cooker. Combine flour, brown sugar and nutmeg in small bowl; sprinkle over carrots and apples. Dot with butter; pour in juice. Cover; cook on LOW 3½ to 4 hours.

Makes 6 servings

Blue Cheese Potatoes

2 pounds red potatoes, peeled and cut into ½-inch pieces

1¼ cups chopped green onions, divided

2 tablespoons olive oil, divided

1 teaspoon dried basil

½ teaspoon salt

¼ teaspoon black pepper

½ cup crumbled blue cheese

1. Layer potatoes, 1 cup green onions, 1 tablespoon oil, basil, salt and pepper in **CROCK-POT®** slow cooker. Cover; cook on LOW 7 hours or on HIGH 4 hours.

2. Gently stir in cheese and remaining 1 tablespoon oil. Cover; cook on HIGH 5 minutes. Remove potatoes to large serving platter; top with remaining ¼ cup green onions.

Makes 5 servings

Slow-Good Apples and Carrots

Cauliflower Soup

2 heads cauliflower, cut into small florets

8 cups vegetable broth

¾ cup chopped celery

¾ cup chopped onion

1 teaspoon salt

2 teaspoons black pepper

2 cups whole milk or light cream

1 teaspoon Worcestershire sauce

1. Combine cauliflower, broth, celery, onion, salt and pepper in **CROCK-POT®** slow cooker. Cover; cook on LOW 7 to 8 hours or on HIGH 3 to 4 hours.

2. Process soup, 1 cup at a time, in food processor or blender until smooth. Return blended soup to **CROCK-POT®** slow cooker after each batch. (Or, use hand-held immersion blender.)

3. Add milk and Worcestershire sauce to food processor; process until blended. Cover; cook on HIGH 15 to 20 minutes until heated through.

Makes 8 servings

Beets in Spicy Mustard Sauce

3 pounds beets, peeled, halved and cut into ½-inch slices

¼ cup sour cream

2 tablespoons spicy brown mustard

2 teaspoons lemon juice

2 cloves garlic, minced

¼ teaspoon black pepper

⅛ teaspoon dried thyme

1. Place beets in **CROCK-POT®** slow cooker. Add enough water to cover by 1 inch. Cover; cook on LOW 7 to 8 hours.

2. Combine sour cream, mustard, lemon juice, garlic, pepper and thyme in small bowl; stir to blend. Spoon over beets; toss to coat. Cover; cook on LOW 15 minutes.

Makes 4 servings

Cauliflower Soup

French Onion Soup

¼ cup (½ stick) butter

3 pounds yellow onions, sliced

1 tablespoon sugar

2 to 3 tablespoons dry white wine or water (optional)

8 cups vegetable broth

8 to 16 slices French bread (optional)

½ cup (2 ounces) shredded Gruyère or Swiss cheese

1. Melt butter in large skillet over medium-low heat. Add onions; cover and cook 10 minutes or just until onions are tender and transparent, but not browned.

2. Remove cover. Sprinkle sugar over onions; cook and stir 8 to 10 minutes or until onions are caramelized. Add onions and any browned bits to **CROCK-POT**® slow cooker. Add wine, if desired, to skillet. Bring to a boil, scraping up any browned bits. Add to **CROCK-POT**® slow cooker. Stir in broth. Cover; cook on LOW 8 hours or on HIGH 6 hours.

3. Preheat broiler. To serve, ladle soup into individual soup bowls. If desired, top each with 1 or 2 bread slices and about 1 tablespoon cheese. Place under broiler until cheese is melted and bubbly.

Makes 8 servings

Variation: Substitute 1 cup dry white wine for 1 cup of vegetable broth.

Slow-Roasted Potatoes

16 small new potatoes

3 tablespoons unsalted butter, cut into small pieces

1 teaspoon paprika

½ teaspoon salt

¼ teaspoon garlic powder

Black pepper

Combine potatoes, butter, paprika, salt, garlic powder and pepper in **CROCK-POT**® slow cooker; stir to blend. Cover; cook on LOW 7 hours or on HIGH 4 hours. Remove potatoes with slotted spoon to large serving dish. Add 1 to 2 tablespoons water to cooking liquid; stir until blended. Pour over potatoes.

Makes 8 servings

French Onion Soup

Red Cabbage and Apples

1 small head red cabbage, cored and thinly sliced

1 large apple, peeled and grated

¾ cup sugar

½ cup red wine vinegar

1 teaspoon ground cloves

Fresh apple slices (optional)

Combine cabbage, grated apple, sugar, vinegar and cloves in **CROCK-POT**® slow cooker; stir to blend. Cover; cook on HIGH 6 hours, stirring halfway through cooking time. Garnish with apple slices.

Makes 6 servings

Rustic Cheddar Mashed Potatoes

2 pounds russet potatoes, diced

1 cup water

2 tablespoons unsalted butter, cubed

¾ cup milk

¾ teaspoon salt

½ teaspoon black pepper

½ cup finely chopped green onions

2 tablespoons shredded Cheddar cheese

1. Combine potatoes, water and butter in **CROCK-POT**® slow cooker. Cover; cook on LOW 6 hours or on HIGH 3 hours. Remove potatoes to large bowl using slotted spoon.

2. Beat potatoes with electric mixer at medium speed 2 to 3 minutes or until well blended. Add milk, salt and pepper; beat 2 minutes or until well blended.

3. Stir in green onions and cheese. Cover; let stand 15 minutes or until cheese is melted.

Makes 8 servings

Red Cabbage and Apples

Barley with Currants and Pine Nuts

1½ teaspoons unsalted butter

1 small onion, finely chopped

2 cups vegetable broth

½ cup uncooked pearl barley

½ teaspoon salt

¼ teaspoon black pepper

⅓ cup currants

¼ cup pine nuts

Melt butter in small skillet over medium-high heat. Add onion; cook and stir 2 minutes or until lightly browned. Remove to **CROCK-POT®** slow cooker. Add broth, barley, salt and pepper to **CROCK-POT®** slow cooker. Stir in currants. Cover; cook on LOW 3 hours. Stir in pine nuts just before serving.

Makes 4 servings

Coconut-Lime Sweet Potatoes with Walnuts

2½ pounds sweet potatoes, cut into 1-inch pieces

8 ounces shredded carrots

¾ cup shredded coconut, toasted and divided*

¼ cup (½ stick) butter, melted

3 tablespoons sugar

½ teaspoon salt

¾ cup walnuts, toasted, coarsely chopped and divided**

2 teaspoons grated lime peel

*To toast coconut, spread evenly on ungreased baking sheet. Toast in preheated 350°F oven 5 to 7 minutes or until light golden brown, stirring occasionally.

**To toast walnuts, spread in single layer in small heavy skillet. Cook and stir over medium heat 1 to 2 minutes or until lightly browned.

1. Combine potatoes, carrots, ½ cup coconut, butter, sugar and salt in **CROCK-POT®** slow cooker. Cover; cook on LOW 5 to 6 hours. Remove to large bowl.

2. Mash potatoes with potato masher. Stir in 3 tablespoons walnuts and lime peel. Sprinkle with remaining walnuts and toasted coconut.

Makes 6 to 8 servings

Barley with Currants and Pine Nuts

Mashed Rutabagas and Potatoes

2 pounds rutabagas, peeled and cut into ½-inch pieces

1 pound potatoes, peeled and cut into ½-inch pieces

½ cup milk

½ teaspoon ground nutmeg

2 tablespoons chopped fresh Italian parsley

Sprigs fresh Italian parsley (optional)

1. Place rutabagas and potatoes in **CROCK-POT**® slow cooker; add enough water to cover vegetables. Cover; cook on LOW 6 hours or on HIGH 3 hours. Remove vegetables to large bowl using slotted spoon. Discard cooking liquid.

2. Mash vegetables with potato masher. Add milk, nutmeg and chopped parsley; stir until smooth. Garnish with parsley sprigs.

Makes 8 servings

Sweet Potato Stew

1 cup chopped onion

1 cup chopped celery

1 cup grated sweet potato

1 cup vegetable broth or water

1 cup half-and-half

Black pepper

¼ cup minced fresh Italian parsley

1. Place onion, celery, sweet potato and broth in **CROCK-POT**® slow cooker. Cover; cook on LOW 6 hours.

2. Turn **CROCK-POT**® slow cooker to HIGH. Add enough half-and-half to **CROCK-POT**® slow cooker to reach desired consistency. Cook, uncovered, on HIGH 30 minutes or until heated through.

3. Season to taste with pepper. Stir in parsley.

Makes 4 servings

Mashed Rutabagas
and Potatoes

Corn on the Cob with Garlic Herb Butter

4 to 5 ears of corn, husked

½ cup (1 stick) unsalted butter, softened

3 to 4 cloves garlic, minced

2 tablespoons finely minced fresh Italian parsley

Salt and black pepper

1. Place each ear of corn on piece of foil. Combine butter, garlic and parsley in small bowl; spread onto corn. Season with salt and pepper; tightly seal foil.

2. Place in **CROCK-POT**® slow cooker, overlapping ears, if necessary. Add enough water to come one fourth of the way up each ear. Cover; cook on LOW 4 to 5 hours or on HIGH 2 to 2½ hours.

Makes 4 to 5 servings

Busy-Day Rice

2 cups water

1 cup uncooked converted rice

2 tablespoons butter

1 tablespoon dried minced onion

1 tablespoon dried parsley flakes

2 teaspoons vegetable bouillon granules

Dash ground red pepper (optional)

Combine water, rice, butter, onion, parsley flakes, bouillon granules and ground red pepper, if desired, in **CROCK-POT**® slow cooker; stir to blend. Cover; cook on HIGH 2 hours.

Makes 4 servings

Variation: During the last 30 minutes of cooking, add ½ cup green peas, broccoli florets or diced carrots.

Corn on the Cob with Garlic Herb Butter

Kale, Olive Oil and Parmesan Soup

2 tablespoons olive oil

1 small Spanish onion, sliced

3 cloves garlic, minced

   Kosher salt and black pepper

8 cups vegetable broth

2 pounds kale, washed and chopped

   Grated Parmesan cheese

   Extra virgin olive oil (optional)

1. Heat olive oil in large, heavy skillet over medium-high heat. Add onion, garlic, salt and pepper; cook and stir 4 to 5 minutes or until onion begins to soften. Remove onion mixture to **CROCK-POT**® slow cooker; add broth. Cover; cook on LOW 3 hours or until heated through.

2. Stir in kale. Turn **CROCK-POT**® slow cooker to HIGH. Cover; cook on HIGH 15 minutes or until heated through. Spoon soup into individual serving bowls. Sprinkle with cheese and drizzle with extra virgin olive oil just before serving.

Makes 4 to 6 servings

Scalloped Tomatoes and Corn

1 can (15 ounces) cream-style corn

1 can (about 14 ounces) diced tomatoes

¾ cup saltine or soda cracker crumbs

1 egg, lightly beaten

2 teaspoons sugar

¾ teaspoon black pepper

   Chopped fresh tomatoes

   Chopped fresh Italian parsley

Combine corn, diced tomatoes, cracker crumbs, egg, sugar and pepper in **CROCK-POT**® slow cooker; stir to blend. Cover; cook on LOW 4 to 6 hours. Sprinkle with fresh tomatoes and parsley just before serving.

Makes 4 to 6 servings

Kale, Olive Oil and Parmesan Soup

Jamaican Quinoa and Sweet Potato Stew

3 cups vegetable broth

1 large or 2 small sweet potatoes (12 ounces), cut into ¾-inch pieces

1 cup uncooked quinoa, rinsed and drained

1 large red bell pepper, cut into ¾-inch pieces

1 tablespoon Caribbean jerk seasoning

¼ cup chopped fresh cilantro

¼ cup sliced almonds, toasted*

Hot pepper sauce or Pickapeppa sauce (optional)

To toast almonds, spread in single layer in heavy skillet. Cook and stir over medium heat 1 to 2 minutes or until nuts are lightly browned.

1. Coat inside of **CROCK-POT**® slow cooker with nonstick cooking spray. Combine broth, potatoes, quinoa, bell pepper and jerk seasoning in **CROCK-POT**® slow cooker; stir to blend.

2. Cover; cook on LOW 5 to 6 hours or on HIGH 2 to 2½ hours. Top each serving with cilantro and almonds. Serve with hot pepper sauce, if desired.

Makes 4 servings

Lemon and Tangerine Glazed Carrots

6 cups sliced carrots

1½ cups apple juice

6 tablespoons butter

¼ cup packed brown sugar

2 tablespoons grated lemon peel

2 tablespoons grated tangerine peel

½ teaspoon salt

Chopped fresh Italian parsley (optional)

Combine carrots, apple juice, butter, brown sugar, lemon peel, tangerine peel and salt in **CROCK-POT**® slow cooker; stir to blend. Cover; cook on LOW 4 to 5 hours or on HIGH 1 to 3 hours. Garnish with parsley.

Makes 10 to 12 servings

Jamaican Quinoa and
Sweet Potato Stew

Metric Conversion Chart

VOLUME MEASUREMENTS (dry)

⅛ teaspoon = 0.5 mL
¼ teaspoon = 1 mL
½ teaspoon = 2 mL
¾ teaspoon = 4 mL
1 teaspoon = 5 mL
1 tablespoon = 15 mL
2 tablespoons = 30 mL
¼ cup = 60 mL
⅓ cup = 75 mL
½ cup = 125 mL
⅔ cup = 150 mL
¾ cup = 175 mL
1 cup = 250 mL
2 cups = 1 pint = 500 mL
3 cups = 750 mL
4 cups = 1 quart = 1 L

VOLUME MEASUREMENTS (fluid)

1 fluid ounce (2 tablespoons) = 30 mL
4 fluid ounces (½ cup) = 125 mL
8 fluid ounces (1 cup) = 250 mL
12 fluid ounces (1½ cups) = 375 mL
16 fluid ounces (2 cups) = 500 mL

WEIGHTS (mass)

½ ounce = 15 g
1 ounce = 30 g
3 ounces = 90 g
4 ounces = 120 g
8 ounces = 225 g
10 ounces = 285 g
12 ounces = 360 g
16 ounces = 1 pound = 450 g

DIMENSIONS

1/16 inch = 2 mm
⅛ inch = 3 mm
¼ inch = 6 mm
½ inch = 1.5 cm
¾ inch = 2 cm
1 inch = 2.5 cm

OVEN TEMPERATURES

250°F = 120°C
275°F = 140°C
300°F = 150°C
325°F = 160°C
350°F = 180°C
375°F = 190°C
400°F = 200°C
425°F = 220°C
450°F = 230°C

BAKING PAN SIZES

Utensil	Size in Inches/Quarts	Metric Volume	Size in Centimeters
Baking or Cake Pan (square or rectangular)	8×8×2	2 L	20×20×5
	9×9×2	2.5 L	23×23×5
	12×8×2	3 L	30×20×5
	13×9×2	3.5 L	33×23×5
Loaf Pan	8×4×3	1.5 L	20×10×7
	9×5×3	2 L	23×13×7
Round Layer Cake Pan	8×1½	1.2 L	20×4
	9×1½	1.5 L	23×4
Pie Plate	8×1¼	750 mL	20×3
	9×1¼	1 L	23×3
Baking Dish or Casserole	1 quart	1 L	—
	1½ quart	1.5 L	—
	2 quart	2 L	—